TAINTED HARVEST
Child Labor and Obstacles to Organizing on Ecuador's Banana Plantations

Human Rights Watch
New York- Washington- London- Brussels

Copyright © April 2002 by Human Rights Watch
All rights reserved
Printed in the United States of America

ISBN: 1-46432-273-4
Library of Congress Catalog Card Number: 2002104124

Cover photo: Copyright © 2001 David Parker
A child banana worker in Ecuador harnessed to a pulley system hauls bananas from the fields to the packing plant.
Cover design by Rafael Jiménez

Addresses for Human Rights Watch
350 Fifth Avenue, 34th Floor, New York, NY 10118-3299
Tel: (212) 290-4700, Fax: (212) 736-1300, E-mail: hrwnyc@hrw.org

1630 Connecticut Avenue, N.W., Suite 500, Washington, DC 20009
Tel: (202) 612-4321, Fax: (202) 612-4333, E-mail: hrwdc@hrw.org

33 Islington High Street, N1 9LH London, UK
Tel: (44 20) 7713 1995, Fax: (44 20) 7713 1800, E-mail: hrwuk@hrw.org

15 Rue Van Campenhout, 1000 Brussels, Belgium
Tel: (32 2) 732-2009, Fax: (32 2) 732-0471, E-mail: hrwbe@hrw.org

Web Site Address: http://www.hrw.org

Human Rights Watch is dedicated to protecting the human rights of people around the world.

We stand with victims and activists to prevent discrimination, to uphold political freedom, to protect people from inhumane conduct in wartime, and to bring offenders to justice.

We investigate and expose human rights violations and hold abusers accountable.

We challenge governments and those who hold power to end abusive practices and respect international human rights law.

We enlist the public and the international community to support the cause of human rights for all.

HUMAN RIGHTS WATCH

Human Rights Watch conducts regular, systematic investigations of human rights abuses in some seventy countries around the world. Our reputation for timely, reliable disclosures has made us an essential source of information for those concerned with human rights. We address the human rights practices of governments of all political stripes, of all geopolitical alignments, and of all ethnic and religious persuasions. Human Rights Watch defends freedom of thought and expression, due process and equal protection of the law, and a vigorous civil society; we document and denounce murders, disappearances, torture, arbitrary imprisonment, discrimination, and other abuses of internationally recognized human rights. Our goal is to hold governments accountable if they transgress the rights of their people.

Human Rights Watch began in 1978 with the founding of its Europe and Central Asia division (then known as Helsinki Watch). Today, it also includes divisions covering Africa, the Americas, Asia, and the Middle East. In addition, it includes three thematic divisions on arms, children's rights, and women's rights. It maintains offices in New York, Washington, Los Angeles, London, Brussels, Moscow, Dushanbe, and Bangkok. Human Rights Watch is an independent, nongovernmental organization, supported by contributions from private individuals and foundations worldwide. It accepts no government funds, directly or indirectly

The staff includes Kenneth Roth, executive director; Michele Alexander, development director; Reed Brody, advocacy director; Carroll Bogert, communications director; John T. Green, operations director, Barbara Guglielmo, finance director; Lotte Leicht, Brussels office director; Michael McClintock, deputy program director; Patrick Minges, publications director; Maria Pignataro Nielsen, human resources director; Malcolm Smart, program director; Wilder Tayler, legal and policy director; and Joanna Weschler, United Nations representative. Jonathan Fanton is the chair of the board. Robert L. Bernstein is the founding chair.

The regional directors of Human Rights Watch are Peter Takirambudde, Africa; José Miguel Vivanco, Americas; Sidney Jones, Asia; Elizabeth Andersen, Europe and Central Asia; and Hanny Megally, Middle East and North Africa. The thematic division directors are Joost R. Hiltermann, arms; Lois Whitman, children's; and LaShawn R. Jefferson, women's.

The members of the board of directors are Jonathan Fanton, Chair; Robert L. Bernstein, Founding Chair, Lisa Anderson, David M. Brown, William Carmichael, Dorothy Cullman, Gina Despres, Irene Diamond, Fiona Druckenmiller, Edith Everett, Michael Gellert, Vartan Gregorian, Alice H. Henkin, James F. Hoge, Jr., Stephen L. Kass, Marina Pinto Kaufman, Wendy Keys, Bruce J. Klatsky, Joanne Leedom - Ackerman, Josh Mailman, Joel Motley, Samuel K. Murumba, Jane Olson, Peter Osnos, Kathleen Peratis, Catherine Powell, Bruce Rabb, Sigrid Rausing, Orville Schell, Sid Sheinberg, Gary G. Sick, Malcolm Smith, Domna Stanton, John Studzinski, Maureen White, Maya Wiley. Emeritus Board: Roland Algrant, Adrian DeWind., and Malcolm Smith.

CONTENTS

I. SUMMARY 1
   Child Workers.. 2
   Freedom of Association... 3
   Corporate Responsibility 5
   Government Obligations... 5

II. GENERAL RECOMMENDATIONS 7

III. BACKGROUND 9
   History of Ecuador Banana Production and Exports 9
   Ecuador Banana Production and Exports Today 11
   Banana-Exporting Corporations 15

IV. CHILD LABOR 20
   Child Labor under International Law 22
   Exposure to Hazardous Substances 24
      Insecticide-treated plastics.. 25
      Applying pesticides in the packing plants 29
      Working during aerial crop fumigation 32
   Work with Dangerous Tools... 38
   Transport of Heavy Loads 39
   Lack of Potable Water and Sanitation 40
   Sexual Harassment 42
   Incomplete Schooling 44
   Child Labor under Domestic Law 47
   Enforcement of Domestic Legal Protections for Child Laborers 49
      Ministry of Labor.. 50
      Juvenile courts 53
      Other governmental bodies 54

V. FREEDOM OF ASSOCIATION... 57
   Freedom of Association under International Law........................... 59
   Freedom of Association under Domestic Law................................ 61
      "Permanent temporary" workers 65
      Use of subcontractors 72
      Weak protections for permanent workers 76

VI. BANANA-EXPORTING CORPORATIONS................................ 79

  Codes of Conduct 83
    Dole 84
    Chiquita 88
    Favorita 92

VII. BANANA EXPORTS AND TRADE REGIMES 95
  European Union Banana Importation Regimes 97

VIII. SPECIFIC RECOMMENDATIONS 101
  To the Government of Ecuador: Preventing the Worst Forms of
    Child Labor 101
  Legal and labor reforms 101
  Enforcement 102
  To the Government of Ecuador: Protecting the Right to
    Freedom of Association 104
  To Banana-Exporting Corporations and Local Suppliers 107
  To the International Labor Organization and the United Nations
    Children's Fund 108
  To Countries Engaged in or Preparing to Engage in Trade with Ecuador ... 110
  To International Financial Institutions 110

APPENDIX A: METHODOLOGY 113

APPENDIX B: LETTERS TO CORPORATIONS 115

APPENDIX C: RESPONSE LETTERS FROM CORPORATIONS 133

ACKNOWLEDGEMENTS

This report was written by Carol Pier, researcher for the Americas Division of Human Rights Watch, based on a three-week fact-finding mission in May 2001. Michael Bochenek, counsel for the Children's Rights Division, participated in a portion of the mission. The report was edited by Bochenek, Jo Becker, advocacy director for the Children's Rights Division, Cynthia Brown, consultant, Arvind Ganesan, director of the Business and Human Rights Program, Joanne Mariner, deputy director of the Americas Division, Malcolm Smart, program director, José Miguel Vivanco, executive director of the Americas Division, and Lois Whitman, executive director of the Children's Rights Division. Research assistance was provided by Ray Mahnad, legal intern. Legal review was performed by Wilder Tayler, legal and policy director. Production assistance was given by Jonathan Balcom and Marijke Conklin, associates for the Americas Division. Technical consultations were provided by Benjamin Davis, Elizabeth O'Connor, and Sonia Rosen of the AFL-CIO's Solidarity Center.

Human Rights Watch is especially grateful to the advocates, activists, and trade unionists who shared their knowledge and experiences with us and, in particular, to those who helped us contact the banana workers interviewed for this report. We also wish to thank the Ecuadorian government officials who provided valuable information regarding Ecuador's labor law regime, the representatives of multilateral organizations who explained their activities and varying degrees of involvement in Ecuador, and employees of banana-exporting corporations—Chiquita, Del Monte, Dole, Favorita, and Noboa—who articulated for us their labor policies on supplier plantations. Finally, we are especially indebted to the many banana workers, children and adults, who shared their stories with us.

I. SUMMARY

When the planes pass, we cover ourselves with our shirts. . . . We just continue working. . . . We can smell the pesticides.

—Enrique Gallana, a fourteen-year-old working on plantation San Carlos in the canton [municipality] of Balao, approximately seventy miles south of Guayaquil in southern Guayas province.

They are fired if they try to unionize. . . . There is not a company that would not fire them. The temporary worker that gets involved in [unionizing] already knows that he's out. . . . Temporary workers are [hired] so as not to have problems with unions. In the moment that the temporary workers unionize, they are fired.

—Martín Insua, minister of labor and human resources of Ecuador.

Roughly one quarter of all bananas on tables in the United States and the European Union are grown on plantations scattered along Ecuador's coast, where workers' international labor rights are flouted daily. Ecuador, the largest banana exporter in the world, whose plantations supply corporations like Dole Food Company, Inc. (Dole), Del Monte Fresh Produce Company (Del Monte), and Chiquita Brands International, Inc. (Chiquita), does not adequately enforce its own labor laws. Nor do those laws fully meet international standards. Ecuadorian children as young as eight labor in banana fields and packing plants where they are exposed to toxic pesticides and other unsafe working conditions in violation of their rights, while adult workers toil in the same hazardous worksites, often with little or no job security, deterred from organizing for fear of summary dismissal. Even Chiquita's own *2000 Corporate Responsibility Report*, analyzing its attempt at socially responsible engagement in Ecuador, recognizes that the country's rise to become the world's leading banana exporter "has been fueled by lower labor, social, and environmental standards than are generally present in the rest of Latin America."

In 2000, roughly 31 percent of Dole's export bananas, 13 percent of Del Monte's, and 7 percent of Chiquita's were supplied by Ecuadorian plantations. In contrast to other Latin American banana-producing countries, where multinational corporations directly own the majority of banana-producing land, in Ecuador, multinationals generally obtain bananas from a multitude of third-party Ecuadorian producers. Of the world's three largest banana corporations—Chiquita, Dole, and Del Monte—only Dole directly owns banana-producing land in Ecuador, approximately 2,000 acres. Similarly,

Ecuador's two largest nationally owned banana-exporting companies, Exportadora Bananera Noboa, S.A. (Noboa), and Rey Banano del Pacífico, C.A. (Reybanpac), the banana-exporting subsidiary of Holding Favorita Fruit Company, Ltd. (Favorita), also rely heavily on third-party producers to supply their export bananas. Thus, exporting corporations, which have foreign sales of over four million metric tons of bananas annually, are able to limit their direct responsibility for the harsh conditions endured by workers producing those bananas. Nonetheless, Human Rights Watch believes that the exporting corporations have an obligation to ensure respect for workers' rights even on their supplier plantations.

In May 2001, Human Rights Watch conducted a three-week fact-finding mission in Quito and the Guayas and El Oro provinces in Ecuador to investigate child labor and obstacles to freedom of association in the banana sector. During the investigation, Human Rights Watch spoke with seventy current and former banana workers, adults and children, whose real names are not used in this report to protect them from potential employer reprisals.

Child Workers

Human Rights Watch interviewed forty-five children who had worked or were working on banana plantations in Ecuador. Forty-one of them began in the banana sector between the ages of eight and thirteen, most starting at ages ten or eleven. They described workdays of twelve hours on average and hazardous conditions that violated their human rights, including dangerous tasks detrimental to their physical and psychological well-being. The children reported being exposed to pesticides, using sharp tools, hauling heavy loads of bananas from the fields to the packing plants, lacking potable water and restroom facilities, and experiencing sexual harassment. Children told Human Rights Watch that they handled insecticide-treated plastics used in the fields to cover and protect bananas, directly applied fungicides to bananas being prepared for shipment in packing plants, and continued working while fungicides were sprayed from planes flying overhead. Sometimes the children were provided protective equipment; most often, they were not. These children enumerated the various adverse health effects that they had suffered shortly after pesticide exposure, including headaches, fever, dizziness, red eyes, stomachaches, nausea, vomiting, trembling and shaking, itching, burning nostrils, fatigue, and aching bones. Children also described working with sharp tools, such as knives, machetes, and short curved blades, and three pre-adolescent girls, aged twelve, twelve, and eleven, described the sexual harassment they allegedly had experienced at the hands of the administrator of two packing plants where they worked. In addition, four boys explained that they attached harnesses to themselves, hooked themselves to pulleys on cables from which banana stalks were hung, and used this pulley system to drag approximately twenty banana-laden stalks, weighing between fifty and one hundred pounds each, over one mile from the fields to the packing plants five or six times a day. Two of these boys stated that, on occasion, the iron pulleys came loose and fell on their heads, making them bleed.

Fewer than 40 percent of these children were still in school at age fourteen. When asked why they had left school to work, most answered that they needed to provide money for their parents to purchase food and clothing for their families, many of whom also relied on the nearby banana plantations for their income. Though important for their families, the average income contributed by the children with whom Human Rights Watch spoke was only U.S. $3.50 for every day worked—roughly 64 percent of the average wage earned by the adults interviewed by Human Rights Watch and 60 percent of the legal minimum wage for banana workers.

If applied, Ecuadorian laws governing child labor could go a long way to protecting the human rights of these children—preventing them from laboring in conditions that violate their right to health and development. If implemented, the laws could also prevent children from engaging in employment likely to interfere with their right to education. Nonetheless, the Ministry of Labor and Human Resources (Ministry of Labor) and the juvenile courts—from which employers must obtain authorization prior to hiring any child under fourteen—fail to fulfill their legally mandated responsibility to enforce domestic laws governing child labor, and the other governmental entities commissioned to address children's issues do not include child banana workers in the scope of their activities. The result is an almost complete breakdown of the government bureaucracy responsible for enforcing child labor laws and preventing the worst forms of child labor in Ecuador's banana sector.

Freedom of Association

In contrast to child labor legislation, Ecuadorian law intended to protect workers' right to freedom of association and to form and join trade unions, even if enforced, is inadequate and fails to deter employers from retaliating against workers for organizing. For example, although the Ecuadorian Constitution and Labor Code guarantee the right to organize, they do not require reinstatement of workers fired for union activity. Instead, an employer need only pay a relatively small fine for an anti-union dismissal, less than U.S. $400 in most cases involving a banana worker.

In addition, Ecuador's failure to enforce its Labor Code provisions governing labor contracts and the ambiguity of those provisions enable employers to create a vulnerable "permanent temporary" workforce in the banana sector. These failures allow for the informal use of consecutive short-term contracts and multiple project contracts. Temporary contracts are strung together, one after the other, for many months or years on end, to create a precarious "permanent temporary" workforce. These "permanent temporary" workers are not entitled to benefits due workers recognized as permanent in the eyes of the law. Because they are not permanent, they have no legal expectation that their jobs will extend beyond the few days or weeks for which they are officially hired. Therefore, their employers are not bound by Labor Code provisions that prohibit anti-union dismissals—if temporary workers are suddenly told not to return to work the following day or week, they have not technically been fired; they have simply not been rehired. And the Labor Code does not explicitly prohibit anti-union discrimination in rehiring.

Finally, the use of subcontracted labor, frequently in work teams with fewer than the thirty workers required by law to form a workers' organization, has also erected often prohibitive obstacles to worker organization. Like "permanent temporary" workers, subcontracted workers, if temporary, lack employment stability. In addition, however, subcontracted workers have no legal right to organize and then collectively bargain with the companies or employers benefiting from their labor—though the companies may determine their wages, benefits, and working conditions. These subcontracted workers are, instead, able to organize and negotiate collectively only with their subcontractors.

Workers with whom Human Rights Watch spoke understood that their right to freedom of association is not, in practice, protected by the Labor Code. The risks inherent in organizing were very clear to workers, particularly temporary workers, and they described a pervasive climate of fear in the sector that deterred them and others from organizing—fear of dismissal and of being labeled "troublemakers."

So strong is the deterrent that banana worker organizing in Ecuador has largely been stifled, and the constitutionally and internationally protected right to freedom of association has been rendered a fiction for most in the sector. So great are the impediments to and risks in exercising the right to freedom of association that, prior to the organizing drive begun in late February 2002 and still underway at this writing, the last concerted attempt to organize banana workers occurred as much as five years ago. Workers have successfully organized on only roughly five of the more than 5,000 registered banana plantations in Ecuador. Only approximately 1,650 of the roughly 120,000 to 148,000 banana workers are affiliated with workers' organizations—

approximately 1 percent of the workforce—a banana worker affiliation rate far lower than that of Colombia or any Central American banana-exporting country.

Corporate Responsibility

These labor rights abuses underlie the production of millions of metric tons of bananas supplied to exporting corporations every year. They occur because of Ecuador's failure to enforce its labor laws and its lack of sufficient legal protections for workers' rights—governmental omissions that allow banana producers to violate workers' rights with impunity. Exporting corporations contract directly with these national producers and benefit from these violations by receiving goods produced under abusive labor conditions. Nonetheless, representatives of Dole, Chiquita, Del Monte, Noboa, and Favorita with whom Human Rights Watch spoke in Ecuador all disclaimed any obligation to demand respect for workers' rights on third-party plantations from which they purchase bananas for export. They explained, in some cases contradicting their own codes of conduct, that supplier plantations are private property over which they have no jurisdiction and that decisions regarding labor matters thereon are ultimately the prerogative of the plantations' administrators. Human Rights Watch believes that when exporting corporations fail to use their financial influence to demand respect for labor rights on their supplier plantations, the exporting corporations benefit from, facilitate, and are therefore complicit in labor rights violations.

Government Obligations

By failing to enforce its child labor laws and its compulsory education requirements in the banana sector, Ecuador has breached its legal obligations under the Convention on the Rights of the Child, the International Labor Organization (ILO) Convention Concerning the Prohibition and Immediate Elimination of the Worst Forms of Child Labour (Worst Forms of Child Labour Convention), and the ILO Minimum Age Convention. Lacking explicit protections against sexual harassment, Ecuadorian law also fails to fulfill the country's obligations under the Convention on the Elimination of All Forms of Discrimination against Women (CEDAW) and the Inter-American Convention on the Prevention, Punishment and Eradication of Violence Against Women (Convention of Belém do Pará). And by failing to give effect to banana workers' right to organize, instead legislatively permitting impediments to freedom of association, Ecuador has violated its duty to respect, protect, and promote workers' right to organize, as required by the International Covenant on Civil and Political Rights (ICCPR), the ILO Convention concerning Freedom of

Association and Protection of the Right to Organise, and the ILO Convention concerning the Right to Organise and Collective Bargaining.

II. GENERAL RECOMMENDATIONS

To remedy Ecuador's failure to comply with its international legal obligations and to address the direct actions of banana-exporting corporations and local banana producers that enable them to benefit from this failure, Human Rights Watch makes the following general recommendations listed below as well as specific recommendations set forth at this report's conclusion.

Recommendation: The Ministry of Labor should fulfill its responsibility to enforce laws governing and relevant to child labor and to develop policies and programs addressing the human rights of child workers. In particular, Ecuador should allocate additional resources to the Ministry of Labor to provide for a sufficient number of labor inspectors to guarantee effective implementation of child labor laws in the banana sector, and the National Committee for the Progressive Elimination of Child Labor should coordinate with other relevant governmental bodies commissioned to address children's issues to develop initiatives targeting child banana workers.

Recommendation: In compliance with the Worst Forms of Child Labour Convention requirement that countries "take effective and time-bound measures to . . . ensure access to free basic education," the constitutional and Minors' Code provisions mandating free and compulsory education for all children under fifteen should be given effect. Mandatory school, book, and uniform fees should be waived or scholarship programs developed for children whose families are unable to afford them; the Labor Code should be amended to increase the fine for employing children who have not reached the legal minimum age for employment, in violation of Ecuadorian law; and a portion of the punitive fine imposed on employers by the Ministry of Labor or juvenile courts should be dedicated to the rehabilitation of the child workers.

Recommendation: Making the letter of the Labor Code conform with its spirit, Congress should amend the Labor Code to prohibit explicitly the use of consecutive temporary contracts and project contracts to create a vulnerable and precarious "permanent temporary" workforce lacking effective protection against anti-union discrimination. The Labor Inspectorate should ensure that the prohibition is effectively enforced.

Recommendation: In accordance with the ILO Committee on Freedom of Association finding that international law protection against anti-union discrimination covers both the dismissal and the recruitment and hiring period, Congress should amend the Labor Code to prohibit explicitly employer failure to hire a worker due to her involvement in or suspected support for organizing activity and should establish adequate and meaningful penalties to deter employers from engaging in anti-union hiring discrimination as well as anti-union dismissals. The Labor Inspectorate should ensure that these protections are effectively enforced.

Recommendation: All banana-exporting corporations, in coordination with their independent local suppliers, should ensure that international labor rights are respected on supplier plantations. Corporations should adopt effective monitoring systems to verify that labor conditions on these plantations comply with internationally recognized workers' rights and relevant national labor laws. In cases where the plantations fall short of such standards, the corporations should provide the economic and technical assistance necessary to bring the local plantations into compliance. The status of such efforts should be reported publicly at least on an annual basis.

III. BACKGROUND

History of Ecuador Banana Production and Exports
Ecuador entered the banana trade in 1910.[1] The country did not become a significant exporter of bananas in the world market, however, until after World War II when Ecuador turned to bananas to fill the void left by the 1920 collapse of its cacao industry.[2] The postwar banana boom began in 1948, when then-President Galo Plaza initiated a program to foster banana industry development that included government agricultural credits, construction of ports and a coastal highway, price regulation, and disease control assistance.[3] Government support for the banana industry did not exist to the same extent in Central America, the dominant Latin American banana-producing region in the prewar years. Such government support, combined with favorable environmental factors—such as the absence of hurricanes, cyclones, and disease, all common in Central America—and banana worker wages significantly lower than in Central America, helped Ecuador become the world's largest banana exporter by 1952.[4] By 1964, Ecuador supplied 25 percent of the world's bananas—more than all Central American banana-producing countries combined.[5]

Due largely to the significant government investment in the banana industry, small and medium-sized local producers were able to enter the industry in Ecuador between the late 1940s and early 1960s.[6] Though to a lesser extent than in Central America, multinational corporations were also directly invested in banana-producing land in Ecuador during this period. Most notably, in 1934,

---

[1] Julian Roche, *The International Banana Trade* (Cambridge, England: Woodhead Publishing Limited, 1998), p. 170.

[2] Banco Central del Ecuador, *El Ecuador de la Postguerra: Estudios en Homenaje a Guillermo Pérez Chiriboga* [*Post-War Ecuador: Studies in Honor of Guillermo Pérez Chiriboga*] (Quito: Banco Central del Ecuador, 1992), p. 151; Carlos Larrea Maldonado, "Los Cambios Recientes en el Subsistema Bananero Ecuatoriano y sus Consecuencias Sobre los Trabajadores: 1977-1984" ["Recent Changes in the Ecuadorian Banana Subsystem and its Consequences for Workers: 1977-1984"], in *Cambio y Continuidad en la Economía Bananera* [*Change and Continuity in the Banana Economy*] (San José, Costa Rica: Facultad Latinoamericana de Ciencias Sociales (FLACSO), Centro de Estudios Democráticos de América Latina, 1988), p. 165.

[3] Banco Central del Ecuador, *El Ecuador de la Postguerra:* . . . , p. 186.

[4] In 1969, wages of banana workers in Ecuador were said to be 42 percent lower than wages of Central American banana workers. Ibid., p. 180.

[5] Carlos Larrea Maldonado, ed., *El Banano en el Ecuador: Transnacionales, Modernización y Subdesarrollo* [*The Banana in Ecuador: Transnationals, Modernization and Underdevelopment*] (Quito: Corporación Editora Nacional, 1987), p. 45.

[6] Banco Central del Ecuador, *El Ecuador de la Postguerra:* . . . , pp. 176-177, 186-187.

the United Fruit Company, later to become Chiquita Brands International, Inc. (Chiquita), purchased plantation Tenguel,[7] an estimated 3,071 hectares (7,677.5 acres) of banana-producing land that alone accounted for approximately 6 percent of Ecuador's banana exports.[8]

As occurred on many other plantations, however, Tenguel's banana plants fell victim to the Panama disease, a devastating fungal infection that appeared in Ecuador in the late 1950s. By 1960, most of the plants had been destroyed. United Fruit dismissed hundreds of workers, cut wages, and eliminated previously provided services. Frustrated workers formed a workers' organization and, later, realizing that little hope remained for future employment under similar conditions, formed a cooperative—an organization responding to the growing peasant agrarian reform movement. On March 27, 1962, the workers invaded Tenguel and seized the land. The state intervened, and United Fruit Company abandoned the zone. Tenguel's downfall was part of a process of contentious agrarian reform, beginning in Ecuador in the 1960s and lasting roughly a decade, that resulted in state-sponsored fragmentation of the large, often unionized, banana plantations owned by multinational corporations into smaller non-union plantations owned by local producers.[9]

Though major factors, agrarian reform and the arrival of the Panama disease were not the only forces behind the flight of foreign banana corporations from Ecuador in the early and mid-1960s. The Cavendish, a new variety of banana, more efficient to produce and more hurricane- and disease-resistant, began replacing other varieties in Central America,[10] effectively negating Ecuador's comparative advantage.[11] Ecuador became a reserve rather than principal supplier, and both those multinational corporations directly owning land and those purchasing bananas from local suppliers either disappeared from or significantly reduced their participation in the Ecuadorian market. The United Fruit Company, for example, by 1965, no longer directly owned any land in Ecuador and only sporadically purchased fruit to cover shortfalls. The Standard Fruit Company, later Dole Food Company, Inc. (Dole), was the

---

[7] Steven Striffler, "Wedded to Work: Class Struggles and Gendered Identities in the Restructuring of the Ecuadorian Banana Industry," 6(1) *Identities: Global Studies in Culture and Power* 91 (1999), pp. 92, 96.

[8] Larrea Maldonado, ed., *El Banano en el Ecuador:* . . . , p. 116.

[9] Striffler, "Wedded to Work: . . . ," p. 102-106.

[10] Larrea Maldonado, ed., *El Banano en el Ecuador:* . . . , p. 156-157.

[11] Ibid., p. 156; Larrea Maldonado, "Los Cambios Recientes en el Subsistema Bananero Ecuatoriano y sus Consecuencias Sobre los Trabajadores . . . ," p. 165.

exception—not owning land directly but never letting its share of Ecuador's international banana market fall below 15 percent.[12]

Ecuador did not fully recover from this crisis until the mid-1970s, when the Standard Fruit Company and Del Monte Fresh Produce Company (Del Monte) decided to make the nation a primary supplier. A variety of factors allegedly contributed to the shift back to Ecuador, including an outbreak of Sigatoka Negra, a costly banana disease, in Central America and Colombia; an export tax levied by the Union of Banana Exporting Countries, which included all significant Latin American banana exporters, minus Ecuador; political unrest in Central America; and heightened union activity in Central America, contributing to a general rise in workers' wages between 1973 and 1976.[13]

Ecuador Banana Production and Exports Today

In contrast to other Latin American banana-producing countries, where multinational corporations directly own approximately 60 percent of banana-producing land,[14] the world's three largest multinational banana corporations—Chiquita, Dole, and Del Monte—still do not own any significant expanse of land in Ecuador. Of these three corporations, only Dole directly owns land—2,000 acres.[15] Thus, their land holdings total only approximately 1 percent of the approximately 147,909 hectares (369,773 acres) of banana-producing land registered with Ecuador's Ministry of Agriculture and Cattle Raising (Ministry of Agriculture).[16] Instead, these corporations obtain bananas

---

[12] Larrea Maldonado, ed., *El Banano en el Ecuador:* . . . , p. 75.

[13] Ibid., pp. 76, 80; Larrea Maldonado, "Los Cambios Recientes en el Subsistema Bananero Ecuatoriano y sus Consecuencias Sobre los Trabajadores . . . ," pp. 81, 172; David Glover and Carlos Larrea Maldonado, "Changing Comparative Advantage, Short Term Instability and Long Term Change in the Latin American Banana Industry," 16 *Canadian Journal of Latin American and Caribbean Studies* 91 (1991), p. 96.

[14] Roche, *The International Banana Trade* . . . , p. 117.

[15] Dole Food Company, Inc., "Form 10-K: Annual Report Pursuant to Section 13 or 15(d) of the Securities Exchange Act of 1934 for the Fiscal Year Ended December 30, 2000," filed March 31, 2001, p. 7.

[16] Ministry of Agriculture, Banana Unit, "Catastro de Productores a Diciembre 2000" ["Registry of Producers to December 2000"], May 2001. Although the Ministry of Agriculture had 5,983 "producers" registered in 2000, Human Rights Watch believes that, in practice, the data reflect the number of banana-producing plantations, not producers or owners, as many of these "producers" appear numerous times in the Ministry of Agriculture's list. Furthermore, according to the National Corporation of Banana Producers (CONABAN), there were 4,800 banana "producers" in 2000. CONABAN-Ecuador, "La Industria Bananera: Perfil del sector productor bananero" ["The Banana Industry: Profile of the banana producer sector"], May 2001, pp. 7, 9.

through a variety of contract arrangements with third-party producers, ranging from exclusive associate producer relationships to sporadic contracts executed to satisfy specific shipment orders. As has historically been the case in Ecuador, these third-party producers range from small, family-owned and -operated plantations of a few acres to medium-sized plots of land to large plantations of more than a thousand acres.[17]

Approximately 99 percent of banana-producing land in Ecuador is concentrated in three provinces in the lowlands of the Pacific coast—El Oro, Guayas, and Los Ríos—where the humid, tropical climate combined with rich soil makes the region ideal for this purpose.[18] The three provinces cover roughly 32,790 square kilometers (some 13,116 square miles), approximately 12 percent of Ecuador's territory, and are home to around 3.4 million people, over a quarter of Ecuador's total population.[19] Excluding residents of Guayaquil, Ecuador's largest city, over one third of those living in the three provinces reside in rural areas,[20] where they work on plantations producing not only bananas but a variety of other crops, including coffee, cocoa beans, sugarcane, rice, and tropical fruits. Conservative estimates suggest that between roughly 120,000 and 148,000 Ecuadorians labor in the country's banana fields and packing plants.[21]

---

[17] Human Rights Watch did not interview any workers laboring on these family-run plantations but, instead, focused its investigation on medium-size and larger plantations. According to Minister of Labor and Human Resources (Minister of Labor) Martín Insua, plantations under thirty hectares (approximately seventy-five acres) are categorized as small, between thirty and sixty hectares (approximately seventy-five acres and 150 acres) as medium, and over sixty hectares (approximately 150 acres) as large. Human Rights Watch interview, Minister of Labor Martín Insua, Quito, May 23, 2001. Human Rights Watch was able to ascertain the approximate number of hectares of sixteen of the twenty-five plantations on which the children interviewed for this report labored. Of those sixteen, fifteen would be classified as large plantations according to the minister's criteria.

[18] Ministry of Agriculture, Banana Unit, "Catastro de Productores a Diciembre 2000."

[19] The Embassy of Ecuador. (No date). *General Information*. [Online]. Available: http://www.embajada-ecuador.se/Info.html [August 20, 2001]; Ecuador on Line. (1999). *Provincia El Oro*. [Online]. Available: http://www.explored.com.ec/ecuador/oro.html [June 29, 2001]; Ecuador on Line. (1999). *Provincia Guayas*. [Online]. Available: http://www.explored.com.ec/ecuador/guayas.html [June 29, 2001]; Ecuador on Line. (1999). *Provincia Los Ríos*. [Online]. Available: http://www.explored.com.ec/ecuador/rios.html [June 29, 2001].

[20] Ecuador on Line. (1999). *Provincia El Oro*. [Online]; Ecuador on Line. (1999). *Provincia Guayas*. [Online]; Ecuador on Line. (1999). *Provincia Los Ríos*. [Online].

[21] There are approximately 147,909 hectares (roughly 369,773 acres) of banana plantations in Ecuador. Ministry of Agriculture, Banana Unit, "Catastro de Productores a Diciembre 2000." After consulting various sources, including government officials and

Unlike most other agricultural products grown in Ecuador, bananas are harvested year-round, usually weekly. Therefore, the myriad tasks performed during the banana production process—beginning when a banana plant sprouts from the root where its parent plant was cut and ending approximately one year later when its fruit is harvested and loaded onto a truck—also usually occur on a weekly basis throughout the year.[22] In the field, banana workers' tasks include weed cutting, applying weed and worm killer, weaving long plastics among bananas to prevent them from damaging each other, covering bananas with insecticide-treated plastic bags, tying insecticide-treated plastic strips around plant stalks, cutting yellowed banana leaves, tying plants to each other or propping them up with wooden poles to ensure stability, tying colored strips around plant stalks to indicate growth phases and monitoring these phases, harvesting fruit-laden stalks and transporting them to the packing plant, and cutting the remaining stems after harvest. In a packing plant—usually nothing more than a shelter with a cement or dirt floor, a roof, and no walls—banana workers, often laboring in small work teams, prepare the fruit for shipment. This preparation process usually lasts between two and four days, depending on the size of the plantation and packing plant. Like field workers, packing plant workers are often assigned discrete tasks, which include removal of plastics from the harvested banana stalks, picking flower remains off the fruit, cutting bananas from their stalks, making banana clusters, discarding bananas that do not meet company standards, washing and weighing the fruit, sticking company labels on each banana cluster, applying post-harvest pesticides, boxing the fruit, loading the boxes onto a truck, and discarding waste from the banana production process.

Today, Ecuador is the world's largest banana exporter. In 2000, the most recent year for which total world-wide banana export figures are available, Ecuador exported 3,993,968 metric tons of the world's 14,155,222 total metric

---

banana corporation representatives, Human Rights Watch learned that a conservative estimate of the ratio of banana workers to plantation hectares is approximately 0.8 to 1, though the ratio may vary depending on various factors, including the technological capacity of a plantation. Human Rights Watch used this ratio to calculate that there are roughly between 120,000 and 148,000 banana workers in Ecuador, understanding "banana worker" as any packing plant or field workers directly involved in the production of bananas.

[22] Human Rights Watch interview, Andrés Arrata, general manager, CONABAN, Guayaquil, May 18, 2001; Banana World. (February 20, 2001). *The fascinating story of the banana.* [Online]. Available: http://home.t-online.de/home/schulz.thomas/story-e.html [August 25, 2001].

tons of banana exports—approximately 28 percent.[23] Bananas are Ecuador's second most important export commodity, following only crude oil, and yield roughly U.S. $900 million annually for the country, accounting for over a quarter of all revenue obtained from trade and approximately 5 percent of Ecuador's gross domestic product.[24] The export bananas are primarily destined for the United States, which in 2000 imported approximately 24 percent of all Ecuadorian banana exports, and the European Union, which in 2000 imported approximately 17 percent.[25]

In 2000, the two leading Ecuadorian banana-exporting corporations—Exportadora Bananera Noboa, S.A. (Noboa), and Rey Banano del Pacífico, C.A. (Reybanpac), the banana-exporting subsidiary of Holding Favorita Fruit Company, Ltd. (Favorita),—grossed approximately U.S. $164.4 million and U.S. $91.3 million respectively.[26] But the combined income of two employed adult banana workers may not be enough to sustain a family. The legal minimum wage for a banana worker in Ecuador working a five-day week is U.S. $117 per month or U.S. $5.85 per day,[27] and the law requires all employers to affiliate workers with Ecuador's Social Security Institute, providing public health insurance.[28] Nonetheless, the average wage of the twenty adult workers who provided Human Rights Watch with their daily wage information was approximately U.S. $5.44, and the vast majority of the workers stated that they

---

[23] United Nations Food and Agriculture Organization (FAO). (No date). *Bananas Exports-Qty (Mt), 2000*. [Online]. Available: http://apps1.fao.org [March 12, 2002]. Ecuador was followed by Costa Rica, Colombia, and the Philippines. According to data provided by CONABAN, Ecuador exported 4,543,556 metric tons of bananas from January through November 2000. CONABAN-Ecuador, "La Industria Bananera: . . . ," p. 12. According to the Ministry of Agriculture, however, Ecuador exported 4,443,069 metric tons of bananas in 2000. Ministry of Agriculture, Banana Unit, "Detalle de Cajas de Banano Exportadas Durante el Año 2000 por País del Destino" ["Detail of Boxes of Banana Exported During the Year 2000 by Country of Destination"].

[24] CONABAN-Ecuador, "La Industria Bananera: . . . ," p. 16; The Embassy of Ecuador. (No date). *General Information*. [Online]; International Monetary Fund (IMF). (May 19, 2000). *Address by Stanley Fischer*. [Online]. Available: http://www.imf.org/external/np/speeches/200/051900.htm [August 25, 2001]; The World Bank Group. (July 2000). *Ecuador Data Profile*. [Online]. Available: http://devdata.worldbank.org [September 8, 2001].

[25] Human Rights Watch telephone interview, Robert Miller, economist, Horticultural and Tropical Products Division, United States Department of Agriculture (USDA), Washington, DC, July 24, 2001.

[26] CONABAN-Ecuador, "La Industria Bananera: . . . ," pp. 16, 22, 24.

[27] Ministry of Labor, Official Registry No. 242 (January 11, 2001).

[28] Labor Code, Article 42(31).

were uninsured.[29] Furthermore, according to Minister of Labor Martín Insua, the basic market basket—the cost of food plus other basic needs—for households in rural Ecuador is approximately U.S. $288 per month.[30] Therefore, in the banana industry, the wages of two working and fully paid adults may not be sufficient to provide for their family, in which case, the added salary of a child may be sought to supplement the family's income. Human Rights Watch found, however, that the majority of children earn even less than adult banana workers. The average daily wage for the forty children who provided Human Rights Watch with their wage information was U.S. $3.50, only 60 percent of the legal minimum wage for banana workers.[31]

Banana-Exporting Corporations

According to the National Corporation of Banana Producers (CONABAN), the following corporations are consistently among the top three banana exporters in Ecuador: Noboa; the Unión de Bananeros Ecuatorianos, S.A. (UBESA), an Ecuadorian subsidiary of Dole; and Reybanpac. In 1999, these three accounted for approximately 56 percent of Ecuador's exports and in 2000, approximately 43 percent.[32] CONABAN data indicate that in 1999, roughly 32 percent and in 2000, approximately 31 percent of Dole's export bananas were supplied by Ecuadorian plantations.[33]

In addition to these corporations, workers with whom Human Rights Watch spoke recounted seeing the brand-name stickers of a number of others adorning the bananas on the plantations where they worked. The two other names most commonly mentioned were Chiquita, represented in Ecuador by its local subsidiary, Brundicorpi, S.A., and Del Monte, represented in Ecuador by its local subsidiary, Bandecua, S.A. Del Monte was the fifth-largest exporter of Ecuadorian bananas in both 1999 and 2000, receiving roughly 14 percent of its export bananas from Ecuador in 1999 and 13 percent in 2000, while Chiquita was the fourth-largest in 1999 and sixth-largest in 2000, receiving

---

[29] Similarly, the IMF has noted that in Ecuador, "[e]nforcement of minimum wages is weak." IMF, "Ecuador: Selected Issues and Statistical Annex," *IMF Staff Country Report No. 00/125* (October 2000), p. 57.

[30] Human Rights Watch interview, Minister of Labor Martín Insua.

[31] Although some workers, both adults and children, reported earning wages on a piece-rate basis, most explained that they were paid a flat rate per day, regardless of production rate or hours worked.

[32] CONABAN-Ecuador, "La Industria Bananera: . . . ," pp. 14, 22, 24.

[33] Ibid., pp. 22, 24.

approximately 17 percent of its export bananas from Ecuador in 1999 but only 7 percent in 2000.[34] In 1999, these five corporations exported approximately 73 percent of all banana exports from Ecuador and in 2000, approximately 52 percent.[35]

The vast majority of the bananas exported by these corporations, however, are not grown on directly owned corporate land, but instead are obtained from third-party suppliers. Chiquita and Del Monte receive 100 percent of their Ecuadorian bananas from third-party suppliers, Dole approximately 98 percent, Noboa between 70 and 80 percent, and Favorita approximately 56 percent.[36] These corporations all have primary suppliers from which they purchase regularly and with which they have close affiliations—as indicated by large signs by the roadside bearing the plantations' names along with corporate logos—and sporadic suppliers from which they purchase occasionally, in most cases, only to fill shipment orders not fully met by the regular suppliers.

Human Rights Watch interviewed forty-five children who had worked or were working on twenty-five different banana plantations in Ecuador—twenty-three in Guayas province and two in El Oro province.[37] Of those twenty-five, sixteen reportedly produce primarily and almost exclusively for Dole and four primarily and almost exclusively for Noboa.[38] Noboa did not respond to Human

---

[34] Ibid.; Human Rights Watch telephone interview, Ricardo Flores, general manager, Brundicorpi, S.A., Guayaquil, July 27, 2001.

[35] CONABAN-Ecuador, "La Industria Bananera: . . . ," pp. 22, 24. According to CONABAN's data, Chiquita's exports from Ecuador fell 58 percent in 2000.

[36] Human Rights Watch interview, Ricardo Flores, Guayaquil, May 24, 2001; Human Rights Watch interview, Marco García, general manager, Bandecua, S.A., Guayaquil, May 24, 2001; Human Rights Watch telephone interview, José Anchundia, director of human resources, UBESA, S.A., Guayaquil, July 10, 2001; Human Rights Watch interview, Francisco Chávez, director of human resources, Noboa, S.A., Guayaquil, May 24, 2001; Human Rights Watch interview, Vicente Wong, executive vice president, Favorita, Ltd., Guayaquil, May 21, 2001; Banana Link. (June 2001). *Noboa.* [Online]. Available: http://www.banalink.org.uk/companies/noboa.htm [July 21, 2001].

[37] Human Rights Watch follows the U.N. Convention on the Rights of the Child in defining as a child "every human being under the age of eighteen unless, under the law applicable to the child, majority is attained earlier." Convention on the Rights of the Child, G.A. Res. 44/25, Annex, 44 U.N. GAOR Supp. (No. 49) at 167, U.N. Doc. A/44/49, November 20, 1989, Article 1.

[38] In some cases, Human Rights Watch observed a sign containing both the corporate logo and the plantation name, strongly suggesting a plantation's primary corporate exporter. This was the case for the following plantations in the canton of Balao in Guayas province that signage strongly suggests produce primarily for Dole: San Fernando, San Alejandro, San Gabriel, and San José, all of the Las Fincas plantation group; Pachina; Porvenir; San José owned by Krapp, S.A.; and San José owned by

Rights Watch's letters seeking to confirm the companies' contractual relationships with these plantations, and Dole refused to confirm or deny its relationships, asserting, "Dole's contractual relationship with its suppliers, the plantations and/or producers with whom Dole has or may have had a relationship is proprietary business information, which Dole does not publicly disclose."[39]

Although none of the twenty-five plantations produces primarily for Chiquita, Del Monte, or Favorita, according to both adult and child banana workers, seventeen occasionally supplied Del Monte, two occasionally supplied Favorita, and fourteen occasionally supplied Chiquita during the years that the children worked there.[40] In a letter to Human Rights Watch, however, Chiquita asserted that during the years in question—1995 through the present—it purchased bananas from only two of these fourteen plantations and denied that it

---

Parazul, S.A. This was also the case for plantation Sociedad Predio Rústico Agrícola Italia in the canton of Balao, which signage strongly suggests produces primarily for Noboa. In other cases, Human Rights Watch relied on the testimony of current and former workers, adults and children, to ascertain a plantation's primary exporter, as is the case with the following plantations that, according to workers, produce primarily for Dole: Recreo in the canton of Naranjal in Guayas province; Predio Rústico La Rural, C.A., or "Pileta," in Balao; Luz Belén in Balao; Italia in Balao; Frutos Bellos, C.A., or "La María," in Balao; El Gran Chaparral in Balao; "Chanique" in Balao; and Balao Chico in Balao. This was also the case for the following plantations in Balao that workers claimed produce primarily for Noboa: Colón, "Paladines," and San Carlos. Human Rights Watch sent a letter to Dole on July 13, 2001 and to Noboa on September 5, 2001 to confirm that these plantations are among their primary suppliers. Noboa did not respond, and Dole asserted that such information is "proprietary business information, which Dole does not publicly disclose." Letter from Freya Maneki, director, corporate communications and shareholder relations, Dole, to Human Rights Watch, October 8, 2001.

[39] Ibid.

[40] The five plantations that signage and testimony suggest primarily supply neither Dole nor Noboa on which one or more children interviewed by Human Rights Watch worked either do not primarily supply any single exporter corporation or primarily supply a smaller company not discussed in this report. These five are Guabital in Balao, San Miguel in Naranjal, Santa Carla in Balao, Cañas owned by Victor Moreno in the canton of Machala in El Oro province, and Cañas owned by Vicente Ortiz in Machala. According to workers, all five produced occasionally for Del Monte, and all but one—Cañas owned by Victor Moreno in Machala—produced sporadically for Chiquita. In addition, workers told Human Rights Watch that on the twenty plantations primarily supplying Dole and Noboa, bananas were produced, on occasion, for other exporters. For example, workers stated that Italia and Balao Chico occasionally supplied Chiquita, Del Monte, and Favorita and that the Las Fincas plantation group, Guabital, Colón, Recreo, San Carlos, Santa Carla, and Sociedad Predio Rústico Agrícola Italia sporadically produced for Chiquita and Del Monte.

purchased any fruit from the plantations in 2000 and 2001.[41] Although Human Rights Watch also sent letters to Del Monte and Favorita inquiring whether the companies had purchased fruit from those plantations on which workers reportedly saw banana stickers with the companies' logos, Del Monte failed to respond and Favorita responded without confirming or denying the contractual relationships.[42]

Correspondingly, of the forty-five children with whom Human Rights Watch spoke, thirty-two stated that, at some time during their short careers, they had worked on plantations primarily supplying Dole and an additional three on plantations that one or more workers alleged occasionally supplied Dole; ten on plantations primarily supplying Noboa and an additional twenty-four on plantations that one or more workers alleged occasionally supplied Noboa; thirty-eight on plantations that one or more workers alleged occasionally supplied Del Monte; fourteen on plantations that one or more workers alleged occasionally supplied Favorita; and thirty-three on plantations that one or more workers alleged occasionally supplied Chiquita. Nonetheless, according to the information provided by Chiquita to Human Rights Watch, Chiquita bought

---

[41] Chiquita denied that from 1995 through the end of June 2001—a period that encompasses the years during which the children interviewed by Human Rights Watch labored as banana workers—it purchased bananas from any of the above-listed plantations, with the exception of Santa Carla and Sociedad Predio Rústico Agrícola. Furthermore, in the cases of Santa Carla and Sociedad Predio Rústico Agrícola, Chiquita asserted that it did not purchase bananas in 2000 or 2001. Letter from Jeffrey Zalla, corporate responsibility officer, Chiquita, to Human Rights Watch, August 28, 2001.

[42] Although Favorita responded to Human Rights Watch's letter, the company did not answer the question of whether it purchased occasionally from plantations Italia and Balao Chico during the years in question. Letter from Dr. Segundo Wong, executive president, Favorita, Ltd., to Human Rights Watch, July 17, 2001.

bananas from plantations that Human Rights Watch determined employed four of those thirty-three children at the time of Chiquita's purchases.[43]

---

[43] Letter from Jeffrey Zalla to Human Rights Watch, August 28, 2001.

IV. CHILD LABOR

Human Rights Watch believes that without reliable government data documenting the scope and scale of child labor in the banana sector, it would be difficult for the government or other institutions to design programs and allocate sufficient resources to remedy violations of child banana workers' human rights. Human Rights Watch, however, was unable to obtain reliable estimates concerning the number of child laborers in Ecuador's banana sector. The Ecuadorian government does not keep such statistics. Although the National Institute of Statistics and Census (INEC) signed an agreement with the International Labor Organization's (ILO) Statistical Information and Monitoring Programme on Child Labour (SIMPOC) in June 2001 to implement a national child labor survey and began the survey in August 2001, this survey will also not disaggregate data by occupation.[44] Other available data, however, provide some guideposts with which to estimate the scope of child labor in the banana sector. In 1994, according to government estimates, approximately 38 percent of all children in Ecuador between the ages of ten and seventeen worked, roughly 808,000 children, approximately 419,000 of whom were between the ages of ten and fourteen.[45] In the rural sector, roughly 59 percent of children between ages ten and seventeen worked, approximately 568,000 children.[46] In 1998, another government survey indicated that the percentage of children at work between the ages of ten and seventeen in Ecuador had risen to 45 percent.[47] There is no breakdown of these figures by industry, however. Based on these statistics assessing the general scope of child labor in Ecuador; Human Rights Watch interviews with seventy current and former child and adult banana workers, most of whom described laboring on plantations alongside other child workers; and the ease with which child banana workers can be found in villages

---

[44] Human Rights Watch telephone interview, Angela Mirtans Oliveira, senior statistician, SIMPOC, Geneva, October 1, 2001.

[45] Mauricio García, *El trabajo y la educación de los niños y de los adolescents en el Ecuador* [*Work and education of children and adolescents in Ecuador*] (Quito: United Nations Children's Fund (UNICEF), 1997), pp. 30-31, citing Servicio Ecuatoriano de Capacitación (SECAP), *Encuesta de Conidiciones de Vida*, 1994 [Ecuadorian Training Service (SECAP), *Survey of Living Conditions*, 1994].

[46] Ibid., pp. 10, 34.

[47] Instituto Nacional del Niño y la Familia; Sistema de Indicadores Sociales sobre los Niños, Niñas y Adolescentes; Secretaría de Estado de Desarrollo Humano; Instituto Nacional de Estadísticas y Censos; Sistema Integrado de Indicadores Socials del Ecuador, *Los Niños y las Niñas del Ecuador* [*Boys and Girls of Ecuador*] (Quito: Ediciones Abya-Yala, 1999), p. 41.

near plantations, Human Rights Watch believes that child labor on banana plantations in Ecuador is widespread.

The forty-five child banana workers—persons under the age of eighteen—with whom Human Rights Watch spoke described the labor conditions under which they worked and the tasks they performed, many of which, under international law, rank their employment among the "worst forms of child labor." They explained that they were exposed to toxic chemicals, handling insecticide-treated plastics, working under fungicide-spraying airplanes in the fields, and directly applying post-harvest pesticides in packing plants. They described using sharp tools, including knives, short curved blades, and machetes, and lacking potable water and sanitation facilities. Four boys explained how they hauled heavy loads of bananas from the fields to the packing plants, and three pre-adolescent girls described experiencing sexual harassment.

When asked why they worked, the vast majority of the children answered that they worked to provide money for their parents to purchase food and clothing for their families. A fourteen-year-old who had worked on plantation Balao Chico in the canton of Balao, approximately seventy miles south of Guayaquil in southern Guayas province, since age twelve succinctly summarized the responses of most children when he explained, "I have to work. There is no money."[48]

The average age at which these forty-five children began working on banana plantations was eleven. Only four started working at age fourteen or above. The other forty-one became banana workers between the ages of eight and thirteen, without prior juvenile court authorization, in violation of both Ecuadorian law and the ILO Minimum Age Convention. Although two of the children indicated that they worked approximately five-hour days, the vast majority worked between nine and thirteen hours a day, with an average workday of eleven hours, also in violation of Ecuadorian law, as well as the ILO

---

[48] Human Rights Watch interview, Bobby Flores, Naranjal, May 12, 2001. According to numerous workers, Balao Chico primarily produces for Dole. One child, Guillermo Guerrero, claimed that he, on occasion, saw the Reybanpac label on bananas produced by Balao Chico; three children, Guerrero, Renato Bermúdez, and Teresa Rivera, and one adult, Nora Ramírez, mentioned that they occasionally saw Del Monte stickers; two children, Guerrero and Bermúdez, reported seeing stickers for Noboa's brand name, Bonita; and one child, Rivera, said that she occasionally saw Chiquita stickers on the bananas produced on Balao Chico. Human Rights Watch interview, Julio Gutiérrez, Guayaquil, May 10, 2001; Human Rights Watch interview, Guillermo Guerrero, Naranjal, May 12, 2000; Human Rights Watch interview, Renato Bermúdez, Naranjal, May 12, 2001; Human Rights Watch interview, Teresa Rivera, Naranjal, May 20, 2001; Human Rights Watch interview, Nora Ramírez, Naranjal, May 20, 2001. Chiquita, however, denied that it purchased bananas from Balao Chico between 1995 and the end of June 2001. Letter from Jeffrey Zalla to Human Rights Watch, August 28, 2001.

Convention concerning the Prohibition and Immediate Elimination of the Worst Forms of Child Labour (Worst Forms of Child Labour Convention), whose recommendation identifies "work under particularly difficult conditions such as work for long hours" as one of "the worst forms of child labor."[49]

Child Labor under International Law

The International Covenant on Civil and Political Rights (ICCPR) states, "Every child shall have . . . the right to such measures of protection as are required by his status as a minor, on the part of his family, society and the State."[50] The Convention on the Rights of the Child provides that children—all persons under eighteen "unless under the law applicable to the child, majority is attained earlier"—have a right "to be protected from performing any work that is likely to be hazardous or to interfere with the child's education, or to be harmful to the child's health or physical, mental, spiritual, moral or social development."[51] All states parties to the convention are required to "undertake all appropriate legislative, administrative, and other measures for the implementation of the rights recognized in this Convention."[52] The Worst Forms of Child Labour Convention expounds on the prohibition of harmful and hazardous work, calling for the elimination of "the worst forms of child labour," defined to include "work which, by its nature or the circumstances in which it is carried out, is likely to harm the health, safety or morals of children."[53] Under the Worst Forms of Child Labour Convention, each state party "shall take immediate and effective measures to secure the prohibition and elimination of the worst forms of child labour as a matter of urgency."[54]

According to the Worst Forms of Child Labour Convention, states parties shall determine what constitutes hazardous work prohibited by the convention in

---

[49] ILO Recommendation concerning the Prohibition and Immediate Elimination of the Worst Forms of Child Labour (Worst Forms of Child Labour Recommendation) (ILO No. R190), June 17, 1999, Article 3(e).

[50] International Covenant on Civil and Political Rights, G.A. Res. 2200A (XXI), 21 U.N. GAOR Supp. (No. 16) at 52, U.N. Doc. A/6316, 999 U.N.T.S. 171, December 16, 1966, Article 24(1). The ICCPR was ratified by Ecuador on March 6, 1969.

[51] Convention on the Rights of the Child, Articles 1, 32(1). Ecuador ratified the Convention on the Rights of the Child on March 23, 1990.

[52] Ibid., Article 4.

[53] ILO Convention concerning the Prohibition and Immediate Elimination of the Worst Forms of Child Labour (ILO No. 182), 38 I.L.M. 1207, June 17, 1999, Article 3(d). Ecuador ratified the Worst Forms of Child Labour Convention on September 19, 2000.

[54] Ibid., Article 1.

consultation with workers' and employers' organizations, considering "relevant international standards, in particular . . . the Worst Forms of Child Labour Recommendation."[55] The recommendation establishes that, in determining the types of work to be considered hazardous, consideration should be given to:

a) work which exposes children to physical, psychological or sexual abuse;
b) work underground, under water, at dangerous heights, or in confined spaces;
c) work with dangerous machinery, equipment and tools, or which involves the manual handling or transport of heavy loads;
d) work in an unhealthy environment which may, for example, expose children to hazardous substances, agents or processes, or to temperatures, noise levels, or vibrations damaging to their health;
e) work under particularly difficult conditions such as work for long hours or during the night or work where the child is unreasonably confined to the premises of the employer.[56]

In addition to establishing a minimum threshold regarding working conditions appropriate for children, the ILO also sets out a minimum age for joining the workforce. The ILO Minimum Age Convention states that the minimum age for admission to employment "shall not be less than the age of completion of compulsory schooling and, in any case, shall not be less than 15 years."[57] An exception to the minimum age of fifteen is made only for "a Member whose economy and educational facilities are insufficiently developed," which may "initially specify a minimum age of 14 years."[58]

---

[55] Ibid., Article 4(1).

[56] Worst Forms of Child Labour Recommendation, Article 3.

[57] ILO Minimum Age Convention (ILO No. 138), June 26, 1973, Article 2(3). The Minimum Age Convention was ratified by Ecuador on September 19, 2000.

[58] Ibid., Article 2(4).

Exposure to Hazardous Substances

> *I went under the packing plant roof until the [fumigation] plane left—less than an hour. I became intoxicated. My eyes were red. I was nauseous. I was dizzy. I had a headache. I vomited.*
>
> —Marcos Santos, describing an event that occurred when he was eleven and working on plantation Guabital in the canton of Balao.[59]

The United States Environmental Protection Agency (U.S. EPA) has recognized that "[c]hildren are at a greater risk for [sic] some pesticides for a number of reasons. Children's internal organs are still developing and maturing and their enzymatic, metabolic, and immune systems may provide less natural protection than those of an adult."[60] Similarly, according to the Natural Resources Defense Council (NRDC), an international environmental nongovernmental organization (NGO), "a sizable body of evidence has shown that children's health is uniquely threatened by environmental hazards."[61] In particular, the NRDC has found that, when in the presence of pesticides, children are proportionately more exposed than adults, due to several factors, including that children's resting breathing rate is significantly higher than resting adults', children have a skin surface area per unit of body weight far greater than adults, and children may be less able than adults to expel toxins from their bodies due to immature kidneys.[62]

Despite the heightened risks they face when exposed to toxic chemicals, most of the child workers with whom Human Rights Watch spoke came into contact with pesticides at one or more stages in the banana production process. Most were never told by employers of the health hazards and dangers of such exposure nor what measures to take to protect themselves from contamination. And in many cases, these often toxic pesticides had been approved for application by the banana-exporting corporations supplied by the plantations on

---

[59] Human Rights Watch interview, Marcos Santos, Naranjal, May 12, 2001.

[60] U.S. EPA. (August 1999). *Protecting Children from Pesticides.* [Online]. Available: http://www.epa.gov/pesticides/citizens/kidpesticide.htrm [July 31, 2001].

[61] NRDC, *Our Children at Risk: The 5 Worst Environmental Threats to Their Health* (New York: NRDC, 1997), chapter 2.

[62] NRDC, *Trouble on the Farm: Growing Up with Pesticides in Agricultural Communities* (New York: NRDC, 1998), chapter 2.

which the children labored, which Human Rights Watch believes makes these corporations highly complicit in the violation of those children's right to health.

Insecticide-treated plastics

The banana production process involves the use of insecticide-treated plastics, which are placed on banana stalks growing in the fields to protect the developing fruit from harmful insects. Most commonly, these insecticides are applied to plastic bags that cover the entire banana stalks, from top to bottom, and to long and thin plastic strips, which are tied around the stalks at each end of the bags. Children reported being involved in placing these treated plastics on the plants, removing them in the packing plants, gathering them from the packing plant floors, and disposing of them.

From lists of the pesticides approved by Chiquita, Dole, and Noboa for use on their directly owned and supplier plantations in Ecuador, provided to Human Rights Watch by representatives of these corporations in Ecuador, Human Rights Watch learned that two of the most common insecticides used in Ecuador to treat the plastics are diazinon and chlorpyrifos. Both insecticides are classified as "moderately hazardous," category II by the World Health Organization (WHO), which measures pesticides' acute risk to human health—the risk caused by exposures over a short period of time—based on their oral and dermal toxicity to rats.[63] According to United Nations Food and Agriculture Organization guidelines, all "moderately hazardous" pesticides should be labeled with a yellow band and the warning, "harmful."[64]

In May through July 2001, chlorpyrifos was deemed a "restricted use product" by the U.S. EPA, and in May 2001, diazinon also appeared on the

---

[63] WHO, *The WHO Recommended Classification of Pesticides by Hazard and Guidelines to Classification 2000-02* (Geneva: WHO, 2001), WHO/PCS/01.5, pp. 2, 21, 22, 53. Depending on their formulation, however, they may be "slightly toxic." Extension Toxicology Network. (March 1, 2001). *Pesticide Information Profile: Diazinon.* [Online]. Available: http://www.pmep.cce.cornell.edu/profiles [July 31, 2001]; Extension Toxicology Network. (March 1, 2001). *Pesticide Information Profile: Chlorpyrifos.* [Online]. Available: http://www.pmep.cce.cornell.edu/profiles [July 31, 2001]. Extension Toxicology Network publications are produced by the Pesticide Information Project of Cooperative Extension Offices of Cornell University, Michigan State University, Oregon State University, and University of California at Davis. Significant funding is provided by the USDA/Extension Service/National Agricultural Pesticide Impact Assessment Program.

[64] FAO, *Guidelines for the management of small quantities of unwanted and obsolete pesticides* (Rome: FAO, 1999), chapter 2.

"restricted use product" list.[65] In June 2000, citing health risks to children, the U.S. EPA reached an agreement with pesticide registrants to phase out certain uses of chlorpyrifos, canceling first "[t]hose uses that pose the most immediate risks to children" and use in schools, parks, and other settings "where children may be exposed."[66] In December 2000, the U.S. EPA similarly announced that the agency had reached an agreement to phase out the use of diazinon because the chemical "is among a class of chemicals . . . which attack the nervous system and are believed to pose special threats to children, even at low doses."[67]

Diazinon and chlorpyrifos are both organophosphates. Originally synthesized in World War II as nerve warfare agents,[68] organophosphates interfere with cholinesterase, "the enzyme [in the brain] that breaks down a critical nerve-impulse-transmitting chemical," causing the over-expression of certain nerve impulses and producing "an array of acute toxic symptoms."[69] Among the symptoms of poisoning are headache, nausea, dizziness, salivation, sweating, wheezing, coughing, tightness in the chest, blurred vision, and in more severe cases, vomiting, diarrhea, abdominal cramps, and slurred speech. At

---

[65] U.S. EPA, Office of Pesticide Programs. (July 11, 2001). *Restricted Use Products Report: Six Month Summary List*. [Online]. Available: http://www.epa.gov/oppmsd1/RestProd/rup6mols.htm [July 31, 2001]. The "restricted use" classification "restricts a product, or its uses, to use by a certified pesticide applicator or under the direct supervision of a certified applicator." U.S. EPA, Office of Pesticide Programs. (July 11, 2001). *Restricted Use Products (RUP) Report*. [Online]. Available: http://www.epa.gov/RestProd/ [September 14, 2001].

[66] U.S. EPA, Office of Pesticide Programs. (June 2000). *Chlorpyrifos Revised Risk Assessment and Agreement with Registrants*. [Online]. Available: http://www.epa.gov/pesticdes [July 31, 2001]. The agreement also sought to "mitigate worker risks" by requiring chlorpyrifos registrants to propose lower application rates, lower frequencies of treatment, and longer periods between applications.

[67] CNN. (December 5, 2000). *EPA phasing out popular ant and roach poison*. [Online]. Available: http://www.cnn.com/200/NATURE/12/05 [August 4, 2001].

[68] Helios Health. (June 13, 2000). *Government Restricts Use of Popular Pesticide*. [Online]. Available: http://www.helioshealth.com/cgi-bin/news [August 4, 2001]; CNN. (December 5, 2000). *EPA phasing out popular ant and roach poison*. [Online]; Andrew C. Revkin, "E.P.A. Sharply Curtails the Use of a Common Insecticide," *New York Times*, June 9, 2000.

[69] NRDC, *Trouble on the Farm* . . . , chapter 1, glossary of terms; J. Routt Reigart, M.D. and James R. Roberts, M.D., M.P.H. (1999). *Recognition and Management of Pesticide Poisonings*. [Online]. Available: http://www.epa.gov/pesticides/safety/healthcare [August 4, 2001], p. 34.

particularly high toxicity levels, seizures, coma, and death may result.[70] Chronic effects may include "impaired memory and concentration, disorientation, severe depressions, irritability, confusion, headache, speech difficulties, delayed reaction times, nightmares, sleepwalking and drowsiness or insomnia."[71] There is also:

> substantial evidence from animal studies that chronic, low-level exposure to organophosphates affects neurodevelopment and neurobehavioral functioning in developing animals. Given this evidence, it is plausible that chronic, low-level exposure to organophosphates adversely affects children's developing nervous systems, possibly resulting in lower cognitive function, behavior disorders, and other subtle neurological deficits.[72]

Because organophosphates can be absorbed through the skin, "dermal contact should be avoided."[73] Skin contact "may cause localized sweating and involuntary muscle contractions" and may lead to other systemic effects, described above.[74]

These organophosphates are two of the insecticides most commonly applied in Ecuador to treat the plastics used in the banana production process. Human Rights Watch, however, could not determine whether these organophosphates were used on the twenty-five plantations on which the forty-five children interviewed labored. Nonetheless, because seventeen of these forty-five children described being in contact with insecticide-treated plastics at one of the stages in the banana production cycle, several anecdotally told of experiencing symptoms of pesticide poisoning after such contact, and each of these organophosphates has been approved by at least one of the five banana-

---

[70] NRDC, *Trouble on the Farm* . . . , chapter 1.; Reigart and Roberts, *Recognition and Management of Pesticide Poisonings*. [Online]. . . . , p. 38; Extension Toxicology Network. (March 1, 2001). *Pesticide Information Profile: Diazinon*. [Online].

[71] Extension Toxicology Network. (March 1, 2001). *Pesticide Information Profile: Chlorpyrifos*. [Online].

[72] Center for Children's Health and the Environment. (2000). *The Pesticide Chlorpyrifos: A Threat to Children*. [Online]. Available: http://www.childenvironment.org/factsheets/chlorpyrifos.htm [July 17, 2001].

[73] Extension Toxicology Network. (March 1, 2001). *Pesticide Information Profile: Chlorpyrifos*. [Online].

[74] Ibid.

exporting corporations discussed in this report, the issue merits further investigation.

Guillermo Guerrero, a fourteen-year-old boy, stated that since he was thirteen, he had been working on Balao Chico tying insecticide-treated plastic strips around the tops and bottoms of banana stalks.[75] He described climbing up a ladder, tying the two strips, climbing down the ladder, and then carrying the ladder to the next plant to repeat the process.[76] Similarly, Carlos Ortiz, a thirteen-year-old boy, explained that, since he was twelve, he had worked in the fields of three plantations in the canton of Balao—Santa Carla, Guabital, and Balao Chico—following a similar procedure to place insecticide-treated plastic bags over banana stalks and tie the treated plastic strips at the stalks' ends.[77]

Several children with whom Human Rights Watch spoke described the effects of handling plastics treated with insecticides. Daniel Ríos, a seventeen-year-old who stated that he had been tying pesticide-treated strips on banana stalks on plantation Balao Chico since he was thirteen, explained, "You can become poisoned from the chemicals. It makes you sick to your stomach and makes you vomit. This happened to me when I was fifteen. . . . My head hurt. I was sick to my stomach."[78] Gregorio Bonilla, a fourteen-year-old boy, stated that recently, while working on the plantation Predio Rústico La Rural, C.A., nicknamed "Pileta," in the canton of Balao, "I got sick working in the fields putting a pesticide-treated plastic strip on the banana stalk. . . . I was not using protective equipment. . . . I had a headache. I was dizzy. I went home. . . . I didn't go to the doctor."[79] Similarly, Carlos Ortiz stated that when he was

---

[75] Human Rights Watch interview, Guillermo Guerrero.

[76] Ibid.

[77] Human Rights Watch interview, Carlos Ortiz, Naranjal, May 12, 2000. According to Ortiz, who told Human Rights Watch that he worked on plantation Santa Carla in 2000, Santa Carla sold sporadically to Del Monte, Noboa, and Chiquita. In a letter to Human Rights Watch, however, Chiquita asserted that it only purchased bananas from Santa Carla in 1999, not in 2000. Letter from Jeffrey Zalla to Human Rights Watch, August 28, 2001. One child, Nicolas Bordón indicated to Human Rights Watch that Guabital also sold sporadically to Del Monte, Noboa, and Chiquita, while another child, Marcos Santos, remembered seeing Del Monte and Chiquita stickers on the bananas produced on Guabital. Human Rights Watch interview, Nicolas Bordón, Naranjal, May 12, 2001; Human Rights Watch interview, Marcos Santos. Chiquita denied that it purchased bananas from Guabital between 1995 and the end of June 2001. Letter from Jeffrey Zalla to Human Rights Watch, August 28, 2001.

[78] Human Rights Watch interview, Daniel Ríos, Naranjal, May 12, 2001.

[79] Human Rights Watch interview, Gregorio Bonilla, Naranjal, May 12, 2001. According to Julio Gutiérrez, a retired banana worker, Predio Rústico La Rural, C.A., primarily produces for Dole, though it occasionally sold fruit to Chiquita as well. Human Rights

eleven and tying insecticide-treated plastic strips on banana stalks on plantation Guabital, "I began to feel bad. . . . My head hurt. . . . I went home."[80]

Many of the children with whom Human Rights Watch spoke, including Carlos Ortiz, stated that they did not use any protective equipment, not even gloves, while handling the treated plastics. Others explained that although they used gloves, they bought them themselves because employers did not provide them. Marta Mendoza, a twelve-year-old girl who had been working since age eleven on the four plantations of Las Fincas in the canton of Balao—San Alejandro, San Fernando, San Gabriel, and San José—told Human Rights Watch that she wore protective gloves to handle insecticide-treated plastics, but "I bought them with my own money. They don't give you any equipment."[81]

Applying pesticides in the packing plants

Children had also been exposed to pesticides when they directly applied fungicides to bananas being prepared for shipment in packing plants—holding small, fungicide-filled tanks and spraying the chemicals through hoses onto the bananas. From the lists of pesticides approved by Chiquita, Dole, and Noboa for use on their directly owned and supplier plantations in Ecuador, Human Rights Watch learned that the most commonly applied pesticides at this stage of production are thiabendazole and imazalil. As with organophosphates, imazalil

---

Watch interview, Julio Gutiérrez, Naranjal, May 19, 2001. Chiquita denied that it purchased bananas from Predio Rústico La Rural, C.A., from 1995 through the end of June 2001. Letter from Jeffrey Zalla to Human Rights Watch, August 28, 2001.

[80] Human Rights Watch interview, Carlos Ortiz.

[81] Human Rights Watch interview, Marta Mendoza, Balao, May 19, 2001; Human Rights Watch interview, Marta Mendoza, Balao, May 26, 2001. The large "Dole" sign, with "Las Fincas" written on the sign underneath the Dole logo, posted outside Las Fincas plantation group, that Human Rights Watch observed and photographed, strongly suggests that the four plantations composing Las Fincas all primarily produce for Dole. Five children also reported that, in addition to Dole stickers, they occasionally saw stickers from Del Monte on the bananas. Human Rights Watch interview, Marta Mendoza, May 19, 2001; Human Rights Watch interview, Violeta Chamorro, Balao, May 19, 2001; Human Rights Watch interview, José Luis Chamorro, Balao, May 19, 2001; Human Rights Watch interview, Carla Chamorro, Balao, May 19, 2001; Human Rights Watch interview, Renato Rodríguez, Balao, May 19, 2001. Three children and an adult also claimed that they occasionally saw Chiquita stickers on the bananas produced by Las Fincas. Human Rights Watch interview, Leonardo Chamorro, Balao, May 19, 2001; Human Rights Watch interview, Renato Rodríguez; Human Rights Watch interview, Violeta Chamorro; Human Rights Watch interview, Rina Castro, Naranjal, May 20, 2001. Chiquita, however, denied that it purchased bananas from any of the Las Fincas plantations between 1995 and the end of June 2001. Letter from Jeffrey Zalla to Human Rights Watch, August 28, 2001.

is classified as "moderately hazardous," category II.[82] It has been found to cause muscle incoordination, reduced arterial tension, tremors, and vomiting,[83] and the International Programme on Chemical Safety, composed of the WHO, the ILO, and the United Nations Environment Programme,[84] has noted that "a harmful concentration of airborne particles can . . . be reached quickly on spraying" and long-term or repeated exposure "may have effects on the liver, resulting in impaired functions and tissue lesions."[85] The product label for imazalil indicates that the chemical may cause "eye damage" and warns, "Do not get in eyes or on clothing. Wear goggles when handling."[86] Thiabendazole, however, is classified by the WHO as "unlikely to present acute hazard in normal use."[87] Despite its WHO classification, thiabendazole, according to the U.S. Occupational Safety and Health Administration, can cause "irritation to the upper respiratory tract" and, if overexposure results, can cause dizziness, nausea, vomiting, headache, weakness, drowsiness, and lack of appetite.[88] Other symptoms, including itching, rashes, and chills, may occur less frequently.[89] According to various product labels in which the active ingredient is thiabendazole, the chemical also causes moderate eye irritation and can be

---

[82] WHO, *The WHO Recommended Classification of Pesticides* . . . , pp. 20, 55.

[83] Extension Toxicology Network. (March 1, 2001). *Pesticide Information Profile: Imazalil*. [Online]. Available: http://www.pmep.cce.cornell.edu/profiles [July 31, 2001].

[84] International Programme on Chemical Safety. (1996). *Copyright Notice and Disclaimers for IPCS INCHEM on the Web*. [Online]. Available: http://www.inchem.org/disclaim.htm [August 4, 2001].

[85] International Programme on Chemical Safety. (1993). *Imazalil*. [Online]. Available: http://www.inchem.org/documents/icsc/icsc/eics1303.htm [August 4, 2001].

[86] Product Label. (June 2, 1986). *Fungaflor*. [Online]. Available: http://oaspub.epa.gov/pestlabl [August 9, 2001].

[87] WHO, *The WHO Recommended Classification of Pesticides* . . . , pp. 36, 58. The Extension Toxicology Network, however, classifies thiabendazole as "slightly toxic," carrying the signal word "caution" on its label. Extension Toxicology Network. (March 1, 2001). *Pesticide Information Profile: Thiabendazole*. [Online]. Available: http://www.pmep.cce.cornell.edu/profiles [July 31, 2001].

[88] United States Department of Labor, Occupational Safety and Health Administration. (November 27, 2000). *Chemical Sampling Information: Thiabendazole*. [Online]. Available: http://www.osha-slc.gov/dts/chemicalsampling/data/CH_271570.htm [July 31, 2001]; see also Extension Toxicology Network. (March 1, 2001). *Pesticide Information Profile: Thiabendazole*. [Online].

[89] Extension Toxicology Network. (March 1, 2001). *Pesticide Information Profile: Thiabendazole*. [Online].

harmful if inhaled or absorbed through the skin, and users should wear rubber gloves and protective clothing when handling.[90]

Although thiabendazole and imazalil are the two pesticides most commonly applied in Ecuador to post-harvest bananas, Human Rights Watch could not verify that they were used on the plantations on which the forty-five children interviewed by Human Rights Watch worked. Nevertheless, fourteen of these children stated that they applied pesticides in the packing plants. One nine-year-old girl told Human Rights Watch that she began applying pesticides when she was eight, working on San Alejandro and San Gabriel of the plantation group Las Fincas.[91]

Several of the children also stated that they did not wear any protective equipment—no gloves, no mask, no goggles, no apron—while applying these chemicals. Humberto Rojas, a fourteen-year-old boy who began as a banana worker at age thirteen, explained, "Sometimes I spray pesticides with the tank in the packing plant. It [the tank] has a hose. I don't [wear] protective equipment. No gloves, no mask." He continued, stating that there was "no orientation. They teach you how to use the tank, [but] only how to use the tank. Nothing about protection."[92] Similarly, Armando Heredia, an eleven-year-old boy, explained that he applied fungicides in a packing plant on plantation San Miguel in the canton of Naranjal, approximately fifty miles south of Guayaquil in southern Guayas province, and that "they don't give you masks. . . . Later, my gloves were damaged, and I began to apply the pesticides with my hands. My dad [had] bought me my gloves. There they don't give them to you."[93]

A number of children described feeling ill after direct exposure to the chemicals applied to the bananas in the packing plants. Ricardo Leiva, a twelve-year-old boy, told Human Rights Watch that when he was eleven, working on a

---

[90] Product Label. (December 30, 1998). *Mertect*. [Online]. Available: http://oaspub.epa.gov/pestlabl [August 9, 2001]; Product Label. (August 7, 1998). *Mertect*. [Online]. Available: http://oaspub.epa.gov/pestlabl [August 9, 2001]; Product Label. (October 30, 1998). *Mertect*. [Online]. Available: http://oaspub.epa.gov/pestlabl [August 9, 2001]; Product Label. (July 27, 1999). *Mertect*. [Online]. Available: http://oaspub.epa.gov/pestlabl [August 9, 2001].

[91] Human Rights Watch interview, Juanita Chamorro, Balao, May 19, 2001.

[92] Human Rights Watch interview, Humberto Rojas, Naranjal, May 12, 2001.

[93] Human Rights Watch interview, Armando Heredia, Naranjal, May 26, 2001. Four children working on San Miguel told Human Rights Watch that they very commonly saw Del Monte stickers on the bananas produced by the plantation. One added, however, that he also occasionally saw Noboa stickers. Ibid.; Human Rights Watch interview, José Santana, Naranjal, May 26, 2001; Human Rights Watch interview, Simón Crúz, Naranjal, May 26, 2001; Human Rights Watch interview, Pablo Castillo, Naranjal, May 26, 2001.

plantation he called "Paladines" in the canton of Balao, "I got sick. . . . I had a headache, fever, [and] cough. I was applying pesticides in the packing plant. The liquid got on my face. I didn't say anything to my boss. I kept on working."[94] Leiva later added, "I never wear gloves. I don't wear anything. They don't give you equipment."[95] Teresa Rivera, a seventeen-year-old girl, stated that for a short time while seventeen she applied fungicides in a packing plant on Balao Chico, wearing an apron, gloves, and mask, but that "when I applied the pesticides, my head hurt. That's why I left there."[96] Marcos Santos, a twelve-year-old boy, explained that he became sick simply from working near pesticide application occurring in a packing plant on Guabital. He explained that, when he was eleven, he was working near pesticide application and "twice I got sick. . . . I vomited. I had a headache. Both times, I went home. The first time, I told the boss. . . . He said, 'Wash your face. Wash your hands. Go home.' The second time, the boss was not there. I went home."[97]

Working during aerial crop fumigation

In addition, children working on banana plantations were exposed to toxic pesticides when they continued laboring in the fields or in packing plants while fungicide-spraying airplanes passed overhead. According to the information provided to Human Rights Watch by representatives of Chiquita, Dole, and Noboa, a variety of different fungicides are sprayed aerially on banana plantations in Ecuador. Based on this information, Human Rights Watch has learned that among the most common are tridemorph, propiconazole, benomyl, mancozeb, azoxystrobin, and bitertanol. The first two are classified as "moderately hazardous," category II by the WHO, while the others are labeled

---

[94] Human Rights Watch interview, Ricardo Leiva, Balao, May 19, 2001. Leiva told Human Rights Watch that he also applied pesticides in the packing plant of San Gabriel, one of the plantations in the Las Fincas plantation group, and that he was also not given any protective equipment on San Gabriel. Workers told Human Rights Watch that "Paladines" primarily produces for Noboa, and Leiva also reported that Dole stickers were occasionally placed on the bananas. Ibid.; Human Rights Watch interview, Timoteo Espinoza, Balao, May 19, 2001; Human Rights Watch interview, Julio Gutiérrez, Naranjal, May 26, 2001. "Paladines" is a nickname that workers have given this plantation, and no one with whom Human Rights Watch spoke knew the plantation's official name.

[95] Human Rights Watch interview, Ricardo Leiva, Balao, May 26, 2001.

[96] Human Rights Watch interview, Teresa Rivera.

[97] Human Rights Watch interview, Marcos Santos.

by the WHO as "unlikely to present acute hazard in normal use."[98] Regardless of their classifications, however, the U.S. EPA has established restricted-entry intervals (REIs)—the time after pesticide application when entry into the treated area is banned or limited—for all aerially applied pesticides, setting a minimum REI of four hours, during which time workers should not be permitted, under any circumstances, to enter treated areas.[99]

Though deemed "unlikely to present acute hazard in normal use," at least three of the latter four fungicides listed above have been found to cause mild adverse health effects. For example, the U.S. EPA has established a twenty-four-hour REI for mancozeb, identified as "moderately irritating to the skin and respiratory mucous membranes," causing itching, scratchy throat, sneezing, coughing, and nose or throat inflammation.[100] The U.S. EPA has also established a twenty-four-hour REI for benomyl and a twelve-hour REI for azoxystrobin,[101] both of which have been found to cause skin reactions and irritation.[102] Benomyl has also been classified by the U.S. EPA as a possible human carcinogen.[103] Furthermore, in the United States, over one hundred

---

[98] WHO, *The WHO Recommended Classification of Pesticides . . .* , pp. 24, 31, 34, 52, 56-58.

[99] Penn State Pesticide Education Office. (No date). *EPA Worker Protection Standard for Agricultural Pesticides.* [Online]. Available: http://www.pested.psu.edu/act12.htm [August 4, 2001]; *2002 Midwest Commercial Small Fruit & Grape Spray Guide.* [Online]. Available: htttp://www.hort.purdue.edu/hort/ext/sfg/default.html [February 4, 2002].

[100] Extension Toxicology Network. (March 1, 2001). *Pesticide Information Profile: Mancozeb.* [Online]. Available: http://www.pmep.cce.cornell.edu/profiles [July 31, 2001]; see also Information Ventures, Inc., for the USDA, Forest Service. (November 1995). *Mancozeb Fact Sheet.* [Online]. Available: http://infoventures.com/e-hlth/pesticide/mancozeb.htm [August 3, 2001]; Reigart and Roberts, *Recognition and Management of Pesticide Poisonings.* [Online]. . . . , p. 144; International Programme on Chemical Safety. (1993). *Mancozeb.* [Online]. Available: http://www.inchem.org/documents/icsc/icsc/eics0754.htm [August 4, 2001].

[101] *2002 Midwest Commercial Small Fruit & Grape Spray Guide.* [Online]; Product Label. (October 9, 1998). *Benlate.* [Online]. Available: http://oaspub.epa.gov/pestlabl [August 9, 2001].

[102] Pesticide Action Network. (March 2001). *Azoxystrobin.* [Online]. Available: http://www.pan-uk.org/pestnews/actives/azoxystr.htm [August 3, 2001]; International Programme on Chemical Safety. (1993). *Benomyl.* [Online]. Available: http://www.inchem.org/documents/icsc/icsc/eics0382.htm [August 4, 2001].

[103] Extension Toxicology Network. (March 1, 2001). *Pesticide Information Profile: Benomyl.* [Online]. Available: http://www.pmep.cce.cornell.edu/profiles [August 3, 2001]. The U.S. EPA classification "possible human carcinogen" connotes "limited evidence of carcinogenicity in the absence of human data." Extension Toxicology

lawsuits from across the world have been filed against the U.S. company producing the benomyl product used on Ecuador's banana plantations, alleging, among other claims, that the chemical is responsible for serious birth defects in children whose parents were exposed to the product, including cleft palate and being born with no eyes.[104] On April 19, 2001, the company announced that it would cease sales of the product on December 31, 2001, though it stated that it "remains fully confident" that the product "is safe when used as directed."[105] Bitertanol is not registered for use in the United States; the U.S. EPA, therefore, has not established an REI for the product, nor have conclusive determinations been made regarding the product's toxicity for humans.[106]

The two "moderately hazardous" fungicides frequently applied to banana crops through aerial fumigation—tridemorph and propiconazole—can cause a variety of unpleasant symptoms. Both have been classified by Germany's Federal Environment Agency as "potential endocrine disrupter[s],"[107] "capable of interfering with the proper functioning of estrogen, androgen and thyroid hormones," which can result in sterility or decreased fertility and metabolic disorders.[108] They have also been found to cause both skin and eye irritation,[109]

Network. (August 31, 1992). *Benomyl (Benlate) NAPIAP Profile on Benomyl 8/92*. [Online]. Available: http://www.pmep.cce.cornell.edu/profiles [August 4, 2001].

[104] Matthew Knowles, "DuPont ditches chemical linked to birth defects," *Associated Newspapers Ltd.*, April 22, 2001; Jan Hollingsworth, "Suits shed light on DuPont's Benlate," *Tampa Tribune*, February 25, 2001; Lois Watson, "Blake talks up future as court battle looms," *Independent Newspapers Ltd.*, August 16, 2001.

[105] DuPont Daily News. (April 19, 2001). *DuPont Statement: DuPont to Phase Out Sale of Benlate*. [Online]. Available: http://www.dupont.com/corp/news/releases/2001/nr04_19_01.html [August 4, 2001].

[106] Human Rights Watch telephone interview, Linda Arrington, ombudsman for the Registration Division, Office of Pesticide Programs, U.S. EPA, Washington, DC, September 21, 2001.

[107] Dr. A. Michael Warhurst, environmental chemist, Friends of the Earth. (July 2000). *Pesticides*. [Online]. Available: http://website.lineone.net/~mwarhurst/pesticides.htm [August 3, 2001], citing ENDS 1999, "Industry Glimpses New Challenges as Endocrine Science Advances," *ENDS Report* 290 (1999), pp. 26-30; Pesticide Action Network. (No Date). *Tridemorph Fact Sheet*. [Online]. Available: http://www.gn.apc.org/pesticidestrust/aifacts/tridemor.htm [August 3, 2001].

[108] Pesticide Action Network Pesticide Database. (May 21, 2001). *Endocrine disrupters*. [Online]. Available: http://www.pesticideinfo.org/documentation3/ref_toxicity5.htm [August 3, 2001].

[109] Information Ventures, Inc., for the USDA, Forest Service. (November 1995). *Propiconazole Fact Sheet*. [Online]. Available: http://infoventures.com/e-hlth/pesticide/propicon.htm [August 3, 2001]; Pesticide Action Network. (June 1999).

and propiconazole has been classified by the U.S. EPA as "a possible human carcinogen."[110] The REI established by the U.S. EPA for propiconazole, according to its product label, is twenty-four hours, while tridemorph has not been registered with the U.S. EPA for use in the United States.[111]

Although these six fungicides are among those most commonly applied aerially to banana plantations in Ecuador, Human Rights Watch cannot verify which, if any, were applied on the plantations on which the forty-five children interviewed by Human Rights Watch labored. However, Human Rights Watch discussed with forty of these children the procedures adopted by their plantations with respect to aerial fumigation. Of the forty, thirty-eight stated that they continued working on the plantations while the airplanes sprayed the banana fields. Diego Rosales, a fourteen-year-old who had worked on plantation Guabital since he was thirteen, explained, "When the plane passes, you keep working. When the water falls on you, you can feel it on your skin. You keep working."[112]

Fifteen of the children who continued working while pesticide-spraying airplanes flew overhead described to Human Rights Watch various adverse health effects that they had suffered after aerial fumigation, including headaches, fever, dizziness, red eyes, stomachaches, nausea, vomiting, trembling and shaking, itching, burning nostrils, fatigue, and aching bones. Although these symptoms of pesticide poisoning could also be attributed to other illnesses, the link between these ailments and the six commonly applied fungicides described in this section—each approved by at least two of the five banana-exporting corporations discussed in this report—merits further investigation.

Fabiola Cardozo said that twice when she was twelve and working in a packing plant on San Alejandro of the plantation group Las Fincas, she became ill after aerial fumigation. She described that the first time, "I got a fever. . . . I told my boss that I felt sick, and he didn't believe me [but] told me to go home. I went home, and my mother took me to the doctor. . . . [The second time,] I

Tridemorph. [Online]. Available: http://www.pan-uk.org/pestnews/actives/tridemor.htm [August 3, 2001].

[110] Information Ventures, Inc., for the USDA, Forest Service. (November 1995). *Propiconazole Fact Sheet.* [Online]; Extension Toxicology Network (March 1, 2001). *Pesticide Information Profile: Propiconazole.* [Online]. Available: http://pmep.cce.cornell.edu/profiles [August 3, 2001].

[111] Product Label. (February 28, 2001). *Tilt.* [Online]. Available: http://oaspub.epa.gov/pestlabl [August 9, 2001]; Human Rights Watch telephone interview, Linda Arrington, U.S. EPA.

[112] Human Rights Watch interview, Diego Rosales, Naranjal, May 12, 2001.

became covered with red things. They itched. I had a cough. My bones hurt. I told my boss. He sent me home. I didn't go to the doctor."[113] Similarly, Carolina Chamorro told Human Rights Watch that after aerial fumigation, "I felt sick twice. I was ten years old. . . . I began to shake." She said that she thought she was going to faint and told her boss, who sent her home, and that her mother took her to the doctor.[114] Susana Gómez, a sixteen-year-old who had worked in a packing plant on Santa Carla in the canton of Balao since she was fourteen, explained that after aerial spraying, "My nose burns. The liquid gets in my nose because of the wind, and my hands begin to itch."[115] Cristóbal Alvarez, a twelve-year-old boy, also explained, "That poison—sometimes it makes one sick. Of course, I keep working. I don't cover myself. Once I got sick. I vomited [and] had a headache . . . after the fumigation. I was eleven years old. . . . I told my bosses. They gave me two days to recover. I went home. The bosses didn't take me to the doctor. My mom took me."[116]

The children told Human Rights Watch about the various methods that they used to protect themselves from the toxic liquid: hiding under banana leaves, bowing their heads, covering their faces with their shirts, covering their noses and mouths with their hands, and placing banana cartons on their heads. As one boy, Enrique Gallana, a fourteen-year-old working on plantation San Carlos in Balao, explained, "When the planes pass, we cover ourselves with our shirts. . . . We just continue working. . . . We can smell the pesticides."[117] Three child packing plant workers and two child field workers also stated that their bosses provided them with masks when the aerial fumigation began but expected them to continue working.[118] Eduardo Martínez, a fourteen-year-old

---

[113] Human Rights Watch interview, Fabiola Cardozo, Balao, May 19, 2001.

[114] Human Rights Watch interview, Carolina Chamorro, Balao, May 19, 2001.

[115] Human Rights Watch interview, Susana Gómez, Naranjal, May 20, 2001.

[116] Human Rights Watch interview, Cristóbal Alvarez, Naranjal, May 12, 2001. When he was eleven, Cristóbal Alvarez was working on plantation Guabital.

[117] Human Rights Watch interview, Enrique Gallana, Balao, May 12, 2001. According to Julio Gutiérrez, the retired banana worker with whom Human Rights Watch spoke, San Carlos primarily produces for Noboa. Gutiérrez and two other children working on San Carlos also mentioned, however, that the plantation produced occasionally for Dole and Del Monte. Human Rights Watch interview, Julio Gutiérrez, Naranjal, May 19, 2001; Human Rights Watch interview, Leonardo Chamorro; Human Rights Watch interview, Carla Chamorro.

[118] Human Rights Watch interview, Fabiola Cardozo; Human Rights Watch interview, Marta Mendoza, May 19, 2001; Human Rights Watch interview, Eduardo Martínez, Naranjal, May 12, 2001; Human Rights Watch interview, Ana López, Naranjal, May 12, 2001; Human Rights Watch interview, Lisa Moreno, Balao, May 27, 2001. Fabiola

who had worked on Balao Chico since he was thirteen, stated, however, that he did not wear the mask provided by his boss and that nobody wore their masks.[119]

Many of the packing plant workers explained that they were shielded by the packing plant roofs from the toxic liquid sprayed from the airplanes. Nevertheless, the packing plants are open-air structures with concrete or dirt floors, roofs on posts, and no walls. Several children correctly observed that, although they were covered by a roof, the fungicide could, nonetheless, be carried through the air into the packing plant's interior. As Armando Heredia, an eleven-year-old working on plantation San Miguel in the canton of Naranjal, explained, "The airplane only passes over the fields, [but] it [the liquid] comes to us with the wind. We cover ourselves with our shirts when the liquid comes."[120] The U.S. EPA has recognized this concept as "spray drift," noting, "When pesticide solutions are sprayed by . . . aircraft, droplets are produced. . . . Many of these droplets can be so small that they stay suspended in air and are carried by air currents."[121]

Cardozo and Marta Mendoza were working in packing plants on the four plantations of Las Fincas. Eduardo Martínez and Ana López both were working in the fields of Balao Chico. Lisa Moreno was working in packing plants on Colón and Pachina. Lisa Moreno and another child worker told Human Rights Watch that Pachina primarily produces for Dole, and Lisa Moreno also stated that she occasionally saw stickers for Del Monte and Noboa on the plantation's bananas. The large sign near plantation Pachina with the name Pachina printed under the Dole corporate logo that Human Rights Watch observed and photographed strongly suggests that Pachina primarily supplies Dole. Juan Luis Alfaro, an adult working on Colón for six years, and two children, Mateo Montoya and Lisa Moreno, told Human Rights Watch that Colón primarily produces for Noboa. Alfaro reported also occasionally seeing stickers for Chiquita and Dole, and Lisa Moreno reported seeing stickers for Del Monte and Dole. Human Rights Watch interview, Juan Luis Alfaro, Balao, May 27, 2001; Human Rights Watch interview, Mateo Montoya, Balao, May 19, 2001; Human Rights Watch interview, Lisa Moreno. Chiquita, however, denied that it purchased bananas from Colón between 1995 and the end of June 2001. Letter from Jeffrey Zalla to Human Rights Watch, August 28, 2001.

[119] Human Rights Watch interview, Eduardo Martínez.

[120] Human Rights Watch interview, Armando Heredia.

[121] U.S. EPA, Office of Pesticide Programs. (February 20, 2001). *Spray Drift of Pesticides.* [Online]. Available: http://www.epa.gov/pesticides/citizens/spraydrift.htm [August 3, 2001].

Work with Dangerous Tools

You cut the piola *with a knife . . . [and] put it in a bag that hangs from a pulley. . . . The pulley is on a cable. . . . The pulley fell on my head. . . . It was loose and fell. I was bleeding and needed five stitches. . . . I was ten.*

—Fabiola Cardozo, describing work in 1999 on San Alejandro of the plantation group Las Fincas.[122]

Children described using sharp knives, machetes, and *curvos*—short, thick, crescent-shaped blades with wooden handles—for a variety of tasks on the plantations. Fifteen children reported handling *curvos*, five machetes, and one a sharp knife used to cut yellow leaves off the banana plants. The children enumerated a variety of uses for the *curvos*, including cutting *piola*—the thick plastic used to stabilize banana plants by tying them to each other; cutting bananas off their stalks; making banana clusters; cutting plastic color-coded ties, used to indicate bananas' stages of development, off the banana stalks; cutting off plastic bags used to cover the banana stalks; and cutting off the long plastics interwoven among bananas to prevent them from damaging each other. They also explained that with the machetes they weeded the fields, cut *piola*, and cut yellow leaves off the banana plants.

Twelve of the children told Human Rights Watch that they had cut themselves with these sharp tools at least once. Cristóbal Alvarez said that in 2001, at age twelve, working on Frutos Bellos, C.A., nicknamed "La María," in the canton of Balao, "I cut myself once. I put up with it. I didn't tell anyone. I put syrup from the banana stalk on it, and there was no more blood."[123] Leonardo Chamorro, a thirteen-year-old boy, similarly explained, "I have cut myself, twice on San José [of the plantation group Las Fincas]. I was twelve. I told the boss that I cut myself, and he sent me home. There was a lot of blood. My mom healed it."[124] Pedro Sandoval also described that when he was thirteen, "I cut myself with a *curvo* on [plantation] Porvenir. I was helping cut

---

[122] Human Rights Watch interview, Fabiola Cardozo.

[123] Human Rights Watch interview, Cristóbal Alvarez. Julio Gutiérrez, the retired banana worker with whom Human Rights Watch spoke, and Cristóbal Alvarez told Human Rights Watch that Frutos Bellos, C.A., primarily produces for Dole. Another little boy agreed but stated that he also, occasionally, saw Noboa stickers. Ibid.; Human Rights Watch telephone interview, Julio Gutiérrez, Guayaquil, July 5, 2001; Human Rights Watch interview, Roberto Pérez, Naranjal, May 12, 2001.

[124] Human Rights Watch interview, Leonardo Chamorro.

bananas off the stalks." He added, "It stayed like this," and he showed Human Rights Watch how the injury had not properly healed.[125] Carla Chamorro, now eleven, also stated, "I cut myself while learning to cut the bananas off the stalk. . . . . I was ten years old. . . . I was working on [the plantation group] Las Fincas."[126]

Transport of Heavy Loads

Four boys told Human Rights Watch that they hauled bananas—approximately twenty full stalks per trip—from the fields to the packing plants. To haul the bananas, a child attaches a harness over his shoulders and around his waist and hooks a wire from his waist to an iron pulley riding on cables, from which the banana stalks are hung on iron wheels. Using this pulley system, a child is able to drag the bananas behind him in the air along the cable as he walks from the field to the packing plant. Carlos Ortiz, a thirteen-year-old, explained that when he was twelve, working on plantation Guabital, he began to haul bananas from the fields using this system. He explained that he pulled twenty banana stalks at once, making about eight trips per day, four days a week. He said, "It weighs a lot."[127] Enrique Gallana, now fourteen, also described that when he was ten, working on plantation Santa Carla, he began hauling bananas to the packing plant, also pulling twenty at a time, making five or six trips—two kilometers (1.25 miles) one way—from the field to the plant, each trip taking about one hour.[128]

When Human Rights Watch asked Guillermo Salgueiro of the Workplace Risks Division of the Ecuadorian Institute for Social Security about the health and safety implications of this practice, Salgueiro replied that the appropriate way to haul bananas from the field to the packing plant is with a mechanized tractor attached to the cables, "not on the ground, because when that person pulls . . . with the body, he suffers problems with the lumbar region."[129] Hauling bananas using the technique described by the four boys, therefore, even if the

---

[125] Human Rights Watch interview, Pedro Sandoval, Balao, May 27, 2001. Sandoval told Human Rights Watch that Porvenir primarily produces for Dole, and Human Rights Watch saw and photographed a sign containing both the Dole corporate logo and the plantation name Porvenir, providing strong evidence corroborating Sandoval's claim.

[126] Human Rights Watch interview, Carla Chamorro.

[127] Human Rights Watch interview, Carlos Ortiz.

[128] Human Rights Watch interview, Enrique Gallana.

[129] Human Rights Watch interview, Guillermo Salguero, engineer, Workplace Risks Division, Ecuadorian Institute for Social Security, Guayaquil, May 17, 2001.

process proceeds smoothly, can cause back injury to the young children dragging the fruit behind them. When the process goes wrong, however, and heavy objects fall from the cables, other severe injuries can occur.

Enrique Gallana told Human Rights Watch that once a stalk of bananas, which can weigh somewhere between fifty and one hundred pounds, fell off the cable and landed on him, knocking him over. Diego Rosales, a fourteen-year-old, explained that three times, "Those things that they use to transport the banana stalks, the iron things they put on the cables, there was one that fell off. It was placed badly, and I didn't realize, and it fell on my head. . . . It breaks the skin and makes you bleed."[130] Carlos Ortiz described a similar experience, stating that when he was twelve, one of the wheels from the cable fell on his head, and "my head split open. Blood came out. I went home, [but] I didn't go to the doctor. I told my boss, and he gave me permission to go home."[131]

Lack of Potable Water and Sanitation

Eighteen children told Human Rights Watch that at least one of the plantations on which they had worked did not have a bathroom for workers to use. Boys explained that, in such situations, if they had to urinate, they went to the banana fields to do so. Three girls, Marta Mendoza, Fabiola Cardozo, and Marta Cárdenas, explained that on San Fernando of the plantation group Las Fincas, there was no bathroom in the packing plant, and "you have to go to the canal to use the bathroom in San Fernando. There is [also] no faucet to wash your hands."[132]

Although most children stated that in the packing plants where they had worked they had access to water they believed to be potable from wells, tanks with chlorine, sink faucets, or hoses, some told Human Rights Watch that there was no potable water for them to drink when they became thirsty while working on the plantations. Several children explained that when they were thirsty, they went home to get water, and four children told Human Rights Watch that when they wanted water, they had to purchase water from small stores on the plantations. Jorge Arrata, a thirteen-year-old who had worked on plantation San José, owned by Parazul, S.A., in the canton of Balao since he was eleven, explained, "There is not water to drink. You have to buy water if you are

---

[130] Human Rights Watch interview, Diego Rosales.

[131] Human Rights Watch interview, Carlos Ortiz.

[132] Human Rights Watch interview, Marta Mendoza, May 19, 2001; Human Rights Watch interview, Marta Cárdenas, Balao, May 19, 2001; Human Rights Watch interview, Fabiola Cardozo.

thirsty. There is a store in the packing plant. . . . It costs [U.S.] $0.25 for a bottle of water."[133]

A few children described drinking water from the runoff canals that travel through the plantations. Guillermo Guerrero, a fourteen-year-old working in the fields of Balao Chico, told Human Rights Watch, "You have to bring water from home in a bottle." If that water runs out, he said, "you have to look for water in the canals. . . . The boss won't give you any."[134] Similarly, Diego Rosales, age fourteen, explained that in the fields of Guabital, where he was working, there was no potable water, only water running in the canals. He told Human Rights Watch that once he broke his arm when he fell into a canal. He said he was thirsty and, like Guillermo Guerrero, was trying to get some water to drink. The canals drain excess water from the fields and catch plantation runoff, including aerially-sprayed fungicides, nematicides sprinkled around the bases of the plants to kill root-eating worms, herbicides sprayed on the ground, fertilizers, and human and animal waste.[135]

Two children also described as "dirty" the water provided to them by the plantations to drink with their lunches. Diego Rosales, who stated that he paid U.S. $0.60 for a lunch consisting of broth, rice, and water from the well, told Human Rights Watch, "There are days when it [the water] is clear. There are days when it is dirty."[136] Enrique Gallana also explained that at plantation San Carlos in the canton of Balao where he was working at age fourteen, he was provided lunch for free but is given water "from the rivers" to drink.[137]

---

[133] Human Rights Watch interview, Jorge Arrata, Balao, May 27, 2001. Arrata told Human Rights Watch that plantation San José, owned by Parazul, S.A., primarily produces for Dole, and Human Rights Watch interviewed the administrator of the plantation, who confirmed this information. Human Rights Watch also saw a sign with the Dole corporate logo and the plantation name San José, Parazul, S.A., printed underneath, strongly suggesting that the plantation primarily supplies Dole.

[134] Human Rights Watch interview, Guillermo Guerrero. Carlos Ortiz also explained that he sometimes drank water from the canals when he was working in the fields because the only potable water was in the packing plant. Human Rights Watch interview, Carlos Ortiz.

[135] See, e.g., Carrie McCracken. (1998). *The Impacts of Banana Plantation Development in Central America.* [Online]. Available: http://members.tripod.com/foro_emaus/BanPlantsCA.htm [September 4, 2001]; Dr. Yamileth Astorga. (1998). *The Environmental Impact of the Banana Industry: A Case Study of Costa Rica.* [Online]. Available: http://www.bananalink.org.uk/impact/impact.htm [September 4, 2001].

[136] Human Rights Watch interview, Diego Rosales.

[137] Human Rights Watch interview, Enrique Gallana.

Sexual Harassment

Human Rights Watch interviewed three young girls, ages twelve, twelve, and eleven, who described being sexually harassed by the "boss" of the packing plants on San Fernando and San Alejandro, plantations of the Las Fincas group. Marta Mendoza, a twelve-year-old who began working on Las Fincas at age eleven, explained, "There is a boss at the plant who's very sick. . . . This man is rude. He goes around touching girls' bottoms. . . . He is in charge there and is always there. He told me that he wants to make love to me. Once he touched me. I was taking off plastic banana coverings, and he touched my bottom. He keeps bothering me. He goes around throwing kisses at me. He calls me 'my love.'" Mendoza added, "He gave my cousin the nickname 'whore.'"[138] Miriam Campos, an eleven-year-old who in 2001 began working on San Fernando and San Alejandro, started to tell Human Rights Watch that "that man" had "said something dirty to me" that "was ugly," but she stopped, looked down at her feet, and said she was too embarrassed to continue.[139] Fabiola Cardozo, a twelve-year-old who began working on Las Fincas at age ten, similarly commented, "The boss of the packing plants . . . says, 'Oh, my love.' When we bend down to pick up plastic bags, he says, '*Alli para meterle huevito.*' ['There is a good place to stick my balls.']" She added that "he says, 'You are going to marry me, and you are going to kiss me.'"[140]

An adult working in the San Fernando and San Alejandro packing plants corroborated the girls' accounts of sexual harassment. When asked about sexual harassment, she responded, "This happens. The little girls, . . . personnel of the administration, heads of the packing plants, quality inspectors . . . bother them. They begin with bad words, . . . vulgar things. The men in the work teams also invite them out, [saying], 'I'll pay you X amount.' . . . There is no respect . . . for them. [They grab] the breasts [and] bottoms of the girls. Some [girls] laugh. Others fight and argue. . . . The boys go around grabbing their breasts and behinds [as well as] people from the company and work colleagues."[141]

The Convention on the Elimination of All Forms of Discrimination against Women (CEDAW) requires states parties to "condemn discrimination against women in all its forms" and "agree to pursue by all appropriate means and

---

[138] Human Rights Watch interview, Marta Mendoza, May 19, 2001.

[139] Human Rights Watch interview, Miriam Campos, Balao, May 19, 2001.

[140] Human Rights Watch interview, Fabiola Cardozo.

[141] Human Rights Watch interview, Sara Portillo, Naranjal, May 20, 2001.

without delay a policy of eliminating discrimination against women."[142] Although CEDAW does not specifically address sexual harassment in the workplace, the Committee on the Elimination of All Forms of Discrimination against Women (CEDAW Committee), which monitors the implementation of CEDAW, has identified sexual harassment as a form of gender-based violence prohibited by the convention. The CEDAW Committee has defined sexual harassment to include:

> such unwelcome sexually determined behavior as physical contact and advances, sexually coloured remarks, showing pornography and sexual demands, whether by words or actions. Such conduct can be humiliating and may constitute a health and safety problem; it is discriminatory when the woman has reasonable ground to believe that her objection would disadvantage her in connection with her employment . . . or when it creates a hostile working environment.[143]

The Inter-American Convention on the Prevention, Punishment and Eradication of Violence Against Women (Convention of Belém do Pará), on the other hand, *explicitly* prohibits sexual harassment, defining violence against women to include violence "that occurs in the community and is perpetrated by any person, including . . . sexual harassment in the workplace."[144] The Convention of Belém do Pará requires and the CEDAW Committee recommends that states parties establish effective measures, including legal sanctions, to prevent such violence and protect women against it.[145]

When the victims of sexual harassment are girls, international law establishes additional protections and prohibits their employment in the hostile work environment created. The Worst Forms of Child Labour Convention

---

[142] Convention on the Elimination of All Forms of Discrimination against Women, G.A. Res. 34/180, 34 U.N. GAOR Supp. (No. 46) at 193, U.N. Doc. A/34/46, December 18, 1979, Article 6. CEDAW was ratified by Ecuador on November 9, 1981.

[143] Committee on the Elimination of Discrimination Against Women, General Recommendation No. 19, A/47/38, 1992, paras. 17, 18.

[144] The Inter-American Convention on the Prevention, Punishment and Eradication of Violence Against Women, OAS/ser.L/II.2.27, CIM/doc.33/94, June 9, 1994, Article 2(b). Ecuador ratified the Convention of Belém do Pará on September 15, 1995. The convention defines violence against women as "any act or conduct, based on gender, which causes death or physical, sexual or psychological harm or suffering to women, whether in the public or private sphere." Ibid., Article 1.

[145] Convention of Belém do Pará, Article 7; CEDAW Committee, General Recommendation No. 19, A/47/38, 1992, para. 24(t).

requires states to "take account of the special situation of girls,"[146] and the Convention on the Rights of the Child prohibits child labor that "is likely to be . . . harmful to the child's health or physical, mental, spiritual, moral or social development."[147] The Worst Forms of Child Labour Recommendation also includes "work which exposes children to physical, psychological or sexual abuse" as one of the "worst forms of child labour" that must be immediately eliminated.[148]

Although Ecuador is a state party to CEDAW, Ecuadorian law does not explicitly prohibit sexual harassment in the workplace nor sex discrimination in employment. Instead, the law sets forth broad discrimination prohibitions. For example, the Constitution establishes a general prohibition of "sex discrimination," providing that "[a]ll people will be considered equal and will enjoy the same rights, freedoms, and opportunities, without discrimination based on . . . sex,"[149] making no specific reference to employment. The Labor Code also fails even to mention employment discrimination, with the exception of the requirement that women and men receive "equal pay for equal work."[150]

Similarly, although Ecuador has ratified both the Convention on the Rights of the Child and the Worst Forms of Child Labour Convention, the Labor Code does not explicitly prohibit employers from placing children in the hostile work environment created by sexual harassment. The Labor Code prohibits employers generally from hiring children to perform jobs that can "be harmful to [the child's] physical, mental, spiritual, moral, or social development," but the law fails to define the scope of this prohibition. To comply with its obligations under international law, Ecuador should explicitly prohibit sexual harassment in the workplace and explicitly prohibit employment of children in the hostile work environment created by sexual harassment.

Incomplete Schooling

The majority of the children with whom Human Rights Watch spoke had quit school before the age of fifteen. Of the forty-two children who began working under the age of fifteen, thirty-seven discussed their schooling with

---

[146] Worst Forms of Child Labour Convention, Article 7(e).

[147] Convention on the Rights of the Child, Article 32(1).

[148] Worst Forms of Child Labour Recommendation, Article 3(a).

[149] Constitution, Article 23(3).

[150] Labor Code, Article 79. The Labor Code also requires employers in each sector to hire a certain minimum percentage of women workers, a percentage established by Sector Commissions of the Ministry of Labor. Ibid., Article 42(34).

Human Rights Watch, and only fourteen—approximately 38 percent—were still in school at age fourteen, working primarily during their vacations.[151] The mother of a fourteen-year-old boy who left school at age thirteen to begin working on plantation Guabital expressed her frustration with the situation, stating, "All of my children work. Working, they're not able to advance. I wish that my children could study, but they can't because they have to work."[152]

Of those still in school, several explained that they often missed school to work. Jorge Arrata, a thirteen-year-old working on plantation San José owned by Parazul, S.A., explained, "I miss one day of school each week."[153] Arrata's mother added with exasperation, "But the teacher does not want to give him permission to work."[154] Three of the children still in school stated that they worked specifically so they could afford to remain in school. A thirteen-year-old who began work at age eleven said, "Almost all the money is for books because there is not enough money for school."[155] Another thirteen-year-old who also began work at age eleven similarly explained, "I save [the money] so I can keep studying."[156]

---

[151] The United States Department of State has noted that, in Ecuador, "[i]n rural areas, many children attend school only sporadically after about 10 years of age in order to contribute to household income as farm laborers." United States Department of State. (February 2001). *Country Reports on Human Rights Practices 2000*. [Online]. Available: http://www.state.gov [September 7, 2001].

[152] Human Rights Watch interview, Diego Rosales' mother, Naranjal, May 12, 2001.

[153] Human Rights Watch interview, Jorge Arrata.

[154] Human Rights Watch interview, Jorge Arrata's mother, Balao, May 27, 2001.

[155] Human Rights Watch interview, Leonardo Chamorro. Leonardo Chamorro was working on plantation San José of plantation group Las Fincas in Balao, plantation San Carlos in Balao, and plantation Sociedad Predio Rústico Agrícola Italia or "Flor María" in Balao. Workers' reports and signage observed by Human Rights Watch strongly suggest that Sociedad Predio Rústico Agrícola Italia primarily produces for Noboa, though three child workers, Violeta Chamorro, Leonardo Chamorro, and Carla Chamorro, reported seeing Dole stickers occasionally placed on the bananas produced by the plantation, and Violeta Chamorro claimed to have seen Del Monte and Chiquita stickers as well. Human Rights Watch interview, Julio Gutiérrez, Naranjal, May 26, 2001; Human Rights Watch interview, Violeta Chamorro; Human Rights Watch interview, Carla Chamorro; Human Rights Watch interview, Leonardo Chamorro. Chiquita acknowledged that from 1997 through 1999, but not during 2000 nor 2001, it purchased bananas from Sociedad Predio Rústico Agrícola Italia. Letter from Jeffrey Zalla to Human Rights Watch, August 28, 2001. Violeta Chamorro told Human Rights Watch that she worked on Sociedad Predio Rústico Agrícola Italia between 1997 and 2001, Leonardo Chamorro from 1999 through 2001, and Carla Chamorro between 2000 and 2001.

[156] Human Rights Watch interview, Jorge Arrata.

The Convention on the Rights of the Child provides that children have a right "to be protected from performing any work that is likely to . . . interfere with the child's education" and recognizes "the right of the child to education."[157] It instructs states parties to "make primary education compulsory and available free to all . . . [and] take measures to encourage regular attendance at schools and the reduction of drop-out rates."[158]

School is mandatory in Ecuador for all children under fifteen and, according to the Constitution, is free through high school.[159] The Minors' Code reiterates that "the State guarantees the right to education . . . [and] basic education is mandatory and free," guaranteeing all children access to basic education.[160] Furthermore, in the case of child workers, employers share the obligation to "ensure that [the child] attends an educational establishment and completes . . . secondary instruction,"[161] and juvenile courts may only grant work authorizations to children ages twelve and thirteen if the children can demonstrate that they have completed or are completing the mandatory minimum schooling.[162]

Nonetheless, work authorizations are rarely sought, and according to a juvenile court judge, even when they are, "in practice, it is not a requirement that school be finished. You receive authorization even if you have not completed [school]."[163] Furthermore, the constitutionally guaranteed "free" public education is undermined by registration and book fees, which, when added to other costs such as uniforms, on average, can total between U.S. $200 and U.S. $250 per student per year,[164] a sum that, according to wage data gathered by Human Rights Watch, would take the average child banana worker roughly between fifty-seven and seventy-one work days to earn. Based on salary information provided by twenty adult banana workers, Human Rights

---

[157] Convention on the Rights of the Child, Articles 32(1), 28(1)(a), (e).

[158] Ibid., Article 28(1)(a), (e).

[159] Constitution, Articles 66, 67.

[160] Minors' Code, Articles 24, 27.

[161] Ibid., Article 156.

[162] Ibid., Article 155(1).

[163] Human Rights Watch interview, Judge Arturo Márquez, Quito Juvenile Court, Quito, May 9, 2001.

[164] Human Rights Watch telephone interview, Lucia Guerra, chief financial administrator, Embassy of Ecuador in the United States, Washington, DC, July 17, 2001.

Watch estimates that families in the banana sector, even if both parents work on plantations, are likely to earn less than U.S. $250 per month.[165]

Child Labor under Domestic Law

Legislation is pending in Ecuador to raise the minimum age of employment to fifteen, the age of completion of mandatory schooling. Currently, however, children between the ages of fourteen and seventeen may work with the express authorization of their parents or other legal representatives.[166] The employment of children under fourteen is prohibited by the Minors' Code, with the exception that juvenile courts may authorize children ages twelve and thirteen to work as apprentices if they have finished primary school.[167] Before granting authorization, a juvenile court must determine that the tasks the apprentice will perform are "compatible with his condition, do not impede continuation of school, and are not noxious for his health."[168]

Under Ecuadorian law, children under eighteen and over fifteen may not work more than seven hours daily or thirty-five weekly and those under fifteen more than six hours daily or thirty weekly. [169] No child may work Sundays or holidays.[170] In addition, adopting language similar to the Convention on the Rights of the Child, the law provides that "the State will protect the minor from economic exploitation and from performing any work . . . that can interfere with

---

[165] According to Guerra, the Ecuadorian government does not provide financial assistance to children unable to afford the fees associated with school matriculation.

[166] Labor Code, Article 35.

[167] Minors' Code, Article 155(1). The ILO Minimum Age Convention allows a country that specifies fourteen as a minimum age of employment, pursuant to article 2(4), to permit the employment of persons ages twelve and thirteen in light work "not likely to be harmful to their health or development" and "not such as to prejudice their attendance at school, their participation in vocational orientation or training programmes approved by the competent authority or their capacity to benefit from the instruction received." ILO Minimum Age Convention, Article 7.

[168] Minors' Code, Article 157. In contrast, the Ecuadorian Labor Code does not restrict the work of children ages twelve or thirteen to apprenticeships and, instead, allows them to work as domestic workers and in other occupations, so long as juvenile courts verify that that they have completed or are completing the mandatory minimum schooling and have "evident need for work" to provide for themselves, parents, or grandparents living with them and unable to work, or younger siblings. Under the Labor Code, employers are required to obtain juvenile court authorization prior to hiring any child under fourteen. Labor Code, Article 134.

[169] Labor Code Article 136.

[170] Ibid., Article 150.

[the child's] education or be harmful to [the child's] physical, mental, spiritual, moral, or social development."[171] The law states that such hazardous work includes "handling psychotropic or toxic objects or substances" and "tasks that are considered dangerous or unhealthy."[172] Limits are also placed on the maximum weight that can be manually transported by children.[173] Demonstrating their compliance with these provisions, employers must maintain special registries with the age, type of work, number of hours worked, salary, and schooling status of each person under eighteen they employ and must send those registries monthly to the Ministry of Labor and Human Resources (Ministry of Labor).[174] If a child nonetheless suffers a workplace illness or accident, despite these precautions and protections, as a result of performing tasks or working under conditions prohibited by law, the employer is presumed responsible, and the indemnity to be received by the child cannot be less than double the ordinary indemnity for such an accident or illness.[175]

The Ministry of Labor, through regional Labor Inspectorates, is responsible for ensuring that employers comply with these and other labor laws.[176] Specifically, "[t]he Ministry of Labor will be responsible for monitoring actions and specific regulations for child labor . . . [,and] [t]he Ministry of Labor will designate one or more Labor Inspectors for Minors . . . in each province."[177] The inspectors "may inspect, at any moment, . . . the conditions in which the work of minors is carried out."[178] Violation of any of

---

[171] Minors' Code, Article 154. The Labor Code similarly prohibits children from working in jobs that "constitute a grave danger to the moral or physical development" of children. Labor Code, Article 138.

[172] Minors' Code, Article 155(2); Labor Code, Article 138.

[173] Labor Code, Article 139. Boys under sixteen are limited to thirty-five pounds, girls under eighteen to twenty pounds, and boys between sixteen and eighteen to fifty pounds. Ibid.

[174] Ibid., Article 147. The registry must be sent to the Labor Directorate and the Director of Employment and Human Resources of the Ministry of Labor.

[175] Ibid., Article 149.

[176] Ibid., Article 553. The Department of Workplace Health and Safety of the Ministry of Labor is assigned to monitor workplaces "to demand compliance with the provisions regarding risk prevention and . . . health and safety." Ibid., Article 563(1); see also Regulation of Worker Health and Safety and Improvement of the Work Environment, Executive Decree 2393, Official Register, November 17, 1986, Article 3(7).

[177] General Regulation to the Minors' Code, Executive Decree 2766, June 7, 1995, Article 64.

[178] Labor Code, Article 151.f

the protections and prohibitions regarding child labor can be punished with a fine of up to U.S. $200 if imposed by the regional Labor Directorate—the body overseeing the regional Labor Inspectorate—and up to U.S. $50 if imposed by labor inspectors or labor courts.[179] Concurrently, a child or her legal representative can also bring a claim before a juvenile court for violation of the child's labor rights, and the court can sanction the violations with fines from one to three times the monthly minimum wage—U.S. $117 to U.S. $351 in the banana sector.[180] Under the Minors' Code, the juvenile courts "will ensure that the rights of the child are integrally respected, preventing exploitation of the minor or violation of [the minor's] rights."[181] In addition, like the Labor Inspectorates, the juvenile courts may "inspect, at any moment, . . . the conditions in which the work of minors is carried out."[182]

Enforcement of Domestic Legal Protections for Child Laborers

If applied, Ecuadorian legislation governing child labor could go a long way to preventing children from laboring in conditions likely to interfere with their right to education or to violate their right to health or development. The legislation could effectively prevent children from performing the worst forms of child labor. Nonetheless, the Ministry of Labor and the juvenile courts fail to fulfill their legally mandated responsibility to enforce the laws governing child labor, and the other governmental entities commissioned to address children's issues fail to include child workers in the banana sector in the scope of their activities.[183]

The result is an almost complete breakdown of the government bureaucracy responsible for enforcing child labor laws and preventing the worst forms of child labor in the banana sector. Ecuador, therefore, is failing to fulfill its international law obligations under the Convention on the Rights of the

---

[179] Ibid., Articles 156, 626

[180] Minors' Code, Article 161; General Regulation to the Minors' Code, Article 67.

[181] Minors' Code, Article 154.

[182] Labor Code, Article 151.f

[183] The IMF has noted the "weakness of enforcement capabilities" for labor legislation in Ecuador. IMF, "Ecuador: Selected Issues and Statistical Annex" . . . , p. 58. Similarly, the United States Department of State found that, in Ecuador, "[i]n practice, the Ministry of Labor fails to enforce child labor laws, and child labor is prevalent." United States Department of State. (February 2001). *Country Reports on Human Rights Practices 2000.* [Online].

Child, the Worst Forms of Child Labour Convention, and the ILO Minimum Age Convention.

Ministry of Labor

When Human Rights Watch asked Berenice Cordero, a United Nations Children's Fund (UNICEF) representative in Ecuador, about government enforcement of Ecuador's child labor laws, she replied, "The Ministry of Labor . . . is focused on other things. . . . It [functions] to resolve conflicts between workers and employers. The ministry . . . is not prepared for this. . . . This whole institutional framework does not function."[184] A representative from the National Institute for Children and Families (INNFA), a primarily state-funded organization complementing government activities on children's issues, similarly explained, "The state does not control it [child labor] at all. . . . At this moment there is nothing to oversee compliance [with child labor laws]. . . . If the [labor] inspectors functioned, it would be different. If what little there is in law were applied, it would be different."[185] He added, "The inspectorate doesn't do it [enforce child labor laws]. . . . [The inspectorate is] for adults, not children."[186]

Silvia Cevallos, director of labor inspectors for the coastal and Galápagos regions, Ecuador's banana-producing zone, explained that, despite the Labor Code requirement, "there are no inspectors for child labor. We take care of that ourselves. When there is a complaint . . . [or] if we have data that there are minors, . . . we send an inspector." Cevallos explained, however, that there are only eleven labor inspectors for the Guayas province, one for El Oro province, and one for Los Ríos province—the nation's three main banana-producing provinces.[187] Too understaffed to carry out meaningful preventative inspections, the Labor Inspectorate must rely on complaints to drive its enforcement of child labor laws.[188] Such a system, however, does not enable the Labor Inspectorate to evaluate, even less to address, the human rights violations suffered by children working on banana plantations, as evidenced by Cevallos' admission to

---

[184] Human Rights Watch interview, Berenice Cordero, UNICEF, Quito, May 7, 2001.

[185] Human Rights Watch interview, Andrés Dueñas, director, Program for the Protection and Education of Working Boys and Girls (PNT), INNFA, Quito, May 7, 2001.

[186] Ibid.

[187] Human Rights Watch interview, Silvia Cevallos, director of labor inspectors for the coastal and Galápagos region, Ministry of Labor, Guayaquil, May 16, 2001.

[188] Human Rights Watch interview, Efraín Duque, director, Labor Directorate for the Coastal and Galápagos Region, Ministry of Labor, Guayaquil, May 16, 2001.

Human Rights Watch—"I have not seen children working in the banana sector."[189] As a result, the Ministry of Labor fails to protect children laboring in the banana sector and is virtually unable to prevent underage children from working.

The Labor Inspectorate's insufficient infrastructure violates Ecuador's obligations under article 10 of the ILO Labour Inspection Convention, which states, "The number of labour inspectors shall be sufficient to secure the effective discharge of the duties of the inspectorate."[190] This violation not only affects the enforcement of child labor provisions but also other protections, such as health and safety norms, whose effective enforcement could go a long way towards eliminating the most egregious violations of child workers' human rights. For example, under Ecuadorian law, all workers, children and adults, must be provided potable water, restrooms, "the equipment necessary to protect them from the risks inherent in the tasks they are performing," and "precise training" on the correct use of that equipment.[191] A representative of the Ecuadorian Social Security Institute, however, bluntly told Human Rights Watch, "The inspectors of the Ministry of Labor do not oversee compliance with health and safety laws. They don't do it."[192] And Dr. Myriam Pozo, working directly for the Minister of Labor in the area of health and safety, explained:

> We don't have a national policy [recognizing] the importance of prevention of risks in work and the obligation to provide healthy and safe conditions. . . . There is no programmed control. . . . To go to a place, perform an inspection, and make recommendations, there are very few teams for this. . . . Labor inspectors do not have the people trained to do these inspections of health and safety. There are two such inspectors . . . in

---

[189] Human Rights Watch interview, Silvia Cevallos.

[190] ILO Labour Inspection Convention (ILO No. 81), July 11, 1947, Article 10. The Labour Inspection Convention was ratified by Ecuador on August 26, 1975.

[191] Regulation of Workers' Safety and Health and Improvement of the Work Environment, Articles 39, 41, 175. In addition, the law specifically instructs banana producers to "install in their packing plants systems of chlorination/purification of water for human consumption." Regulation of Banana Plantation Environmental Health, Decree No. 0093, Official Register No. 406, March 24, 1994, Article 33.

[192] Human Rights Watch interview, Dr. Luis Vásquez, director, National Subdirectorate of Workplace Risks, Ecuadorian Social Security Institute, Quito, May 9, 2001.

the coastal region. . . . There is no time to perform preventive inspections.[193]

When asked about enforcement of laws governing pesticide application, Pozo responded:

> The use of pesticides is our responsibility . . . [but] no one is demanding that the law be complied with. . . . The inspectorate does not know about pesticides. They are not trained for this. They don't know it. . . . We are very poor at this.[194]

The director of the Labor Directorate for the Coastal and Galápagos Region, who oversees the region's Labor Inspectorate, similarly stated that, with respect to pesticide use and handling, while he hopes that the laws are applied, "There is no control. There is no control with respect to labor authorities."[195]

Both producers and workers with whom Human Rights Watch spoke confirmed that government inspectors rarely, if ever, visit banana plantations. One plantation owner, when asked if government inspectors had visited his plantations, said, "No one. No authority. Never. They never visit agricultural properties. . . . The government doesn't demand anything. They have abandoned the worker."[196] The president of the Regional Union of Farmworker Organizations of the Coast (UROCAL), an association of small banana producers, similarly noted that government inspectors "do not come. Only if you call them with an invitation. They never come to inspect. . . . A culture of supervision . . . —that doesn't exist."[197] The general manager of CONABAN, an association of large producers, agreed, adding, "There is no oversight . . . by the Ministry of Labor. . . . They only function by complaint."[198] An official of the Association of Banana Producers Orenses, an association of small and medium-sized banana producers, when asked about enforcement of child labor

---

[193] Human Rights Watch interview, Dr. Myriam Pozo, area of workplace health and safety, Ministry of Labor, Quito, May 23, 2001.

[194] Ibid.

[195] Human Rights Watch interview, Efraín Duque.

[196] Human Rights Watch interview, Bolívar Moreno, banana plantation owner, Machala, May 14, 2001.

[197] Human Rights Watch interview, Joaquín Vásquez, president, UROCAL, Machala, May 15, 2001.

[198] Human Rights Watch interview, Andrés Arrata.

laws, told Human Rights Watch, "As far as I know, in the agricultural sector, they're not applied."[199]

Workers made similar observations. One worker noted, "They [government inspectors] never come. That's why there's abuse."[200] Several workers explained that the only inspectors they ever saw were from banana-exporting corporations visiting plantations to verify fruit quality and production procedures. One commented that there were no government inspectors, "only inspectors of fruit, quality, but they don't worry about our well-being."[201] Of the sixteen adult workers to whom Human Rights Watch posed the question of whether they had ever seen government inspectors enter the banana plantations on which they worked, not one responded in the affirmative.

Juvenile courts

As with the Labor Inspectorate, the juvenile courts lack the institutional capacity to "inspect, at any moment" the conditions in which children are laboring, which they are empowered to do by law, and, therefore, cannot effectively address the human rights violations suffered by child workers.[202] According to Judge Arturo Márquez, from a juvenile court in Quito, "Going to observe, control—this is not a practice that is carried out. The tribunals do not inspect." He added that enforcing laws governing child labor "has not been a [national] priority. Society does not demand it; the state does not demand it, and the courts cannot do it." He explained that he has approximately 8,000 cases every year, saying, "I am smothered by cases. . . . An administrative entity, the Ministry of Labor, . . . should perform . . . these preventive inspections. A judge cannot go around doing that. . . . The [juvenile] justice system does not function, and [the state] continues giving it work that does not correspond to it." Without the infrastructure to make preventive site visits, the overburdened juvenile courts, like the understaffed Labor Inspectorate, rely on complaints submitted to enforce child labor laws and protections. Nevertheless, Judge Márquez told Human Rights Watch, "In the seven years I've been here, there has not been one [case in] which labor rights have been at issue."[203]

---

[199] Human Rights Watch interview, Jorge Topanta, director, publicity and statistics, Association of Banana Producers Orenses, Machala, May 14, 2001.

[200] Human Rights Watch interview, Antonio Romero, Balao, May 27, 2001.

[201] Human Rights Watch interview, Gema Caranza, Guayaquil, May 10, 2001.

[202] Labor Code, Article 151.f

[203] Human Rights Watch interview, Judge Arturo Márquez.

In addition, requests for work authorizations, mandatory for children under fourteen, are rarely filed. According to statistics kept by the juvenile courts, there were a total of 121 work authorizations provided in 2000 in the eight juvenile courts located in Ecuador's three main banana-producing provinces—El Oro, Guayas, and Los Ríos.[204] In Guayas, the region in which all but one of the forty-five child banana workers interviewed by Human Rights Watch worked, there was a total of sixty-seven authorizations for all labor sectors.

Commenting on the work authorization process, Berenice Cordero, the UNICEF representative, stated that the system of juvenile court work authorization "does not function. . . . The employer has no interest in doing these procedures."[205] Judge Márquez added, "Few ask for [work authorization]. Our problem is that there does not exist an authority that demands that employers comply."[206]

Other governmental bodies

In addition to the labor inspectors and the juvenile courts, several governmental bodies have been commissioned to address children's issues, including the National Council for Children and Adolescents, within the Ministry of Social Welfare; the National Directorate for the Protection of Minors, within the Ministry of Social Welfare; and the National Committee for the Progressive Elimination of Child Labor, within the Ministry of Labor.

The National Council for Children and Adolescents does not address child labor. According to Berenice Cordero of UNICEF, rather, it oversees kindergartens, day cares, and rehabilitation centers.[207] Nonetheless, according to the General Regulation for the Minors' Code, the council "is responsible for policies for protection of working minors," in coordination with the National Directorate for Protection of Minors, juvenile courts, and the Ministry of Labor.[208] Under the same regulation, the National Directorate for Protection of Minors, along with the juvenile courts and other local organizations, is asked to "establish . . . programs for protection, defense, and promotion of the rights of

---

[204] "Estadísticas Realizadas en los Diferentes Tribunales de Menores del País, Enero a Diciembre del 2000" ["Statistics Kept in the Different Juvenile Courts in the Country, January to December 2000"].

[205] Human Rights Watch interview, Berenice Cordero.

[206] Human Rights Watch interview, Judge Arturo Márquez.

[207] Human Rights Watch interview, Berenice Cordero.

[208] General Regulation to the Minors' Code, Article 64.

child workers . . . in the rural sector."[209] In practice, the national directorate focuses on abandoned children, and, according to INNFA, has "neither a policy nor action on child labor."[210]

The National Committee for the Progressive Elimination of Child Labor, for its part, has among its legally mandated functions "[t]o approve the National Plan for the Progressive Elimination of Child Labor;" "[t]o promote, organize, assist, and coordinate policies and programs directed to prohibit, restrict, and regulate child labor;" and "[t]o promote compliance with legislation on child labor."[211] When asked about child labor in the banana sector, however, the head of the National Committee for the Progressive Elimination of Child Labor told Human Rights Watch, "In the banana sector, we have not entered very directly. The child labor is hidden. It takes place at the level of the nuclear family. . . . This work has not yet been measured, and we cannot, for now, establish its

---

[209] Ibid., Article 65.

[210] Human Rights Watch interview, Amparo Armas, national technical coordinator, Institutionality Project, INNFA, Quito, May 7, 2001.

[211] Creation of the National Committee for the Progressive Elimination of Child Labor, Decree No. 792.

level." He added that the committee has obtained "results in some sectors, but in the banana sector, we do not have results."[212]

---

[212] Human Rights Watch interview, Dr. Jorge Ortega, director, National Committee for the Progressive Elimination of Child Labor, Ministry of Labor, Quito, May 9, 2001. As mentioned above, none of the forty-five child workers interviewed by Human Rights Watch was working on a plantation owned by his or her family.

V. FREEDOM OF ASSOCIATION

Juan Luis Alfaro, who worked for six years with a permanent contract as a subcontractor for plantation Colón in Balao, told Human Rights Watch that he was fired for requesting a raise for himself and his work team and then accused by his employer of having union sympathies. He explained:

> I spoke with the administrator. I wanted him to recognize the amount of boxes [of bananas we produced] and give us more money. . . . He called the plantation owner on the radio. The owner said that he couldn't do that and that I was a troublemaker and that the administrator should look for another work team. . . . I asked for a raise in the morning. At 5:00 that afternoon, they fired me—me and the whole team. . . . The administrator communicated to me that the owner did not need our services and had another team all ready.[213]

Alfaro continued, "They [then] sent around papers so that they won't give me work on other plantations. Administrators of other plantations showed me the papers. They [the papers] say that I am a troublemaker and that I want to unionize. . . . They don't give me work. They don't want to." He added, "The following day I went to speak to the owner to ask for [indemnity]. He told me that he is not going to recognize not even a cent."[214] At the time of Human Rights Watch's interview with Alfaro, he was working in a bakery, unable to find work on banana plantations in the area.

Employers who retaliate against workers for exercising their right to organize face few, if any, meaningful repercussions under domestic law, as worker reinstatement is not required and fines for illegal dismissals, in most cases, are insignificant. Moreover, legal loopholes allow employers to create a vulnerable, "permanent temporary" workforce without job security, and the use of subcontracted temporary work teams is widespread on banana plantations. These factors have combined to create a climate of fear among banana workers and largely prevent them from organizing.

Julio Gutiérrez, a retired banana worker from Naranjal, explained to Human Rights Watch, "It's the fear they instill in you. . . . You don't affiliate. They fire you."[215] Tomás Peña, a sixty-nine-year-old banana worker who had labored in work teams for thirty-six years on a plantation in Balao, stated,

---

[213] Human Rights Watch interview, Juan Luis Alfaro.
[214] Ibid.
[215] Human Rights Watch interview, Julio Gutiérrez, Guayaquil, May 10, 2001.

"There are no unions. The employers don't want unions.... Knowing that you are involved in a union, they fire you. It is not good for them."[216] Cecilia Menéndez, employed until October 2000 on plantation Colón, stated, "No union. ... They do not let us. When the people begin to get together, ... they are fired for it."[217] Victor Garza, a banana worker in Balao for over forty years, similarly told Human Rights Watch that there are few unions because "when you want to organize and the bosses know it, they fire you. It's the fear we have. We don't have unions because we are afraid."[218]

Substantiating their deep-seated fear of retaliatory dismissal, several workers described cases they recalled of workers who were fired for supporting unionization. Sara Portillo, a worker employed on the plantation group Las Fincas, explained that up until approximately six or seven years ago when the plantation group went bankrupt and was sold, a union existed on the plantations composing Las Fincas. She said, "With the new owner, all the people from Santa Rita [the previous name of the plantation group] who were trade unionists were not given work.... The bosses told the guards not to allow them to work. [If trade unionists entered the plantation,] people who knew them told the guards that they were unionists, and the guards advised the administrator, and they were thrown out."[219] She concluded that people do not attempt unionization now because they fear losing their jobs.

So great are the impediments to and risks in exercising the right to freedom of association that organizing efforts in the sector have been rare. An organizing drive began in February 2002 and is still underway at this writing. Prior to this effort, however, the last concerted attempt to organize banana workers occurred more than five years ago, according to several representatives from the National Federation of Free Farmworkers and Indigenous Peoples of Ecuador (FENACLE) and a representative of the AFL-CIO Solidarity Center in Ecuador.[220] Workers have successfully organized on only roughly five of the

---

[216] Human Rights Watch interview, Tomás Peña, Balao, May 27, 2001. Peña told Human Rights Watch that the plantation on which he worked, whose name Human Rights Watch has omitted to protect Peña's anonymity, primarily produces for Noboa but that he occasionally saw stickers for Dole placed on the bananas.

[217] Human Rights Watch interview, Cecilia Menéndez, Balao, May 27, 2001. According to Francisco Chávez, director of human resources for Noboa, Alamos Rey-Rancho is directly owned by Noboa. Human Rights Watch interview, Francisco Chávez.

[218] Human Rights Watch interview, Victor Garza, Balao, May 19, 2001.

[219] Human Rights Watch interview, Sara Portillo.

[220] Human Rights Watch interview, Franklin Zambrano, secretary general, FENACLE, Naranjal, May 20, 2001; Human Rights Watch interview, Guillermo Touma, president,

more than 5,000 registered banana plantations in Ecuador,[221] and only about 1,650 of the roughly 120,000 to 148,000 banana workers are affiliated—approximately 1 percent.[222] The result is a banana worker affiliation rate far lower than that of Colombia or any Central American banana-exporting country.[223]

Freedom of Association under International Law

The ICCPR states that "everyone shall have the right to freedom of association with others, including the right to form and join trade unions for the protection of his interests,"[224] and the International Covenant on Economic, Social and Cultural Rights (ICESCR) similarly recognizes "[t]he right of everyone to form trade unions and join the trade union of his choice."[225] The ILO Declaration on Fundamental Principles and Rights at Work has recognized freedom of association as one of the "fundamental rights," which all ILO

FENACLE, Quito, May 8, 2001; Human Rights Watch interview Patricio Contreras, Ecuador representative, AFL-CIO's Solidarity Center, Washington, DC, April 24, 2001.

[221] Ibid.

[222] Guillermo Touma and Franklin Zambrano provided Human Rights Watch with estimates of the number of affiliates in each of the five workers' organizations. Human Rights Watch interview, Franklin Zambrano; Human Rights Watch interview, Guillermo Touma.

[223] Although information and data regarding worker organization rates vary, often widely, depending on the source, Human Rights Watch estimates that organization rates in the top five banana-exporting countries in Latin America are: Ecuador at approximately 1 percent; Costa Rica, with the next lowest rate, at between roughly 6 and 7 percent; Colombia and Panama at approximately 90 percent; and Guatemala at roughly 40 percent, with the rate varying significantly depending on the region. Human Rights Watch telephone interview, Efrén Sandovál, Office of the Legal Commission, Sindicato de Trabajadores de Bananeros de Izabal [Union of Banana Workers of Izabal] (SITRABI), Guatemala, June 25, 2001; Human Rights Watch telephone interview, Manuel Marqués, secretary of education, Sindicato de Trabajadores de la Industria Agropecuaria [Union of Workers of the Agriculture and Livestock Industry] (SINTRAINAGRO), Colombia, June 25, 2001; Human Rights Watch telephone interview, Germán Zepeda, director, Coordinadora Latinoamericana de Sindicatos Bananeros [Coordinator of Latin American Banana Unions] (COLSIBA), Honduras, June 25, 2001; Human Rights Watch telephone interview, Gilberth Bermúdez, director, Sindicato de Trabajadores de Plantaciones Agrícolas [Union of Workers of Agriculture Plantations] (SITRAP), Costa Rica, June 25, 2001; U.S./Labor Education in the Americas Project, Issue #2, August 2000, p. 5.

[224] ICCPR, Article 22(1).

[225] International Covenant on Economic, Social and Cultural Rights, G.A. Res. 2200A (XXI), 21 U.N. GAOR Supp. (No. 16) at 49, U.N. Doc. A/6316, 993 U.N.T.S. 171, December 16, 1966, Article 8(1). Ecuador ratified the ICESCR on March 6, 1969.

members have an obligation to respect and promote.[226] The ILO Convention concerning Freedom of Association and Protection of the Right to Organise states, "Workers . . . without distinction whatsoever, shall have the right to establish and . . . to join organizations of their own choosing without previous authorization."[227] The ILO has clarified that "without distinction" means that "workers . . . be they employed on a permanent basis or for a fixed term, have the right to establish and join organizations of their choosing."[228]

The ILO Convention concerning the Right to Organise and Collective Bargaining elaborates on the fundamental right to freedom of association, establishing:

> Workers shall enjoy adequate protection against acts of anti-union discrimination in respect of their employment. . . . Such protection shall apply more particularly in respect of acts calculated to . . . (b) [c]ause the dismissal of or otherwise prejudice a worker by reason of union membership or because of participation in union activities.[229]

According to the ILO Committee on Freedom of Association, protection against anti-union discrimination should cover the periods of recruitment and hiring, employment, and dismissal.[230] The committee has found, however, that

---

[226] International Labour Conference, ILO Declaration on Fundamental Principles and Rights at Work, 86th Session, Geneva, June 18, 1998. According to ILO Declaration on Fundamental Principles and Rights at Work, "all Members, even if they have not ratified the Conventions in question, have an obligation arising from the very fact of membership in the Organization to respect, to promote and to realize, in good faith and in accordance with the Constitution, the principles concerning the fundamental rights which are the subject of those Conventions." Therefore, even countries that have not ratified the ILO Convention concerning Freedom of Association and Protection of the Right to Organise and the ILO Convention concerning the Right to Organise and Collective Bargaining are bound by this obligation.

[227] ILO Convention concerning Freedom of Association and Protection of the Right to Organise (ILO No. 87), 68 U.N.T.S. 17, July 4, 1950, Article 2. ILO Convention No. 87 was ratified by Ecuador on May 29, 1967.

[228] ILO, *Complaint against the government of the Philippines presented by the International Federation of Building and Woodworkers (IFBWW)*, Report No. 292, Case No. 1615, Vol. LXXVII, 1994, Series B, No. 1, para. 332(a).

[229] ILO Convention concerning the Right to Organise and Collective Bargaining (ILO No. 98), 96 U.N.T.S. 257, July 18, 1951, Article 1. ILO Convention No. 98 was ratified by Ecuador on May 28, 1959.

[230] ILO Committee on Freedom of Association, *General (Protection against anti-union discrimination)*, Digest of Decisions, Doc. 1201, 1996, para. 695. The ILO Committee on Freedom of Association examines complaints from workers' and employers'

as long as "adequate protection" during these periods is, in fact, provided, the methods adopted to safeguard workers against anti-union discrimination may vary from country to country.[231] The ILO's Committee of Experts on the Application of Conventions and Recommendations (ILO Committee of Experts) has clarified, however, that because the remedy for anti-union dismissal should "compensate fully, both in financial and in occupational terms, the prejudice suffered by a worker as a result of an act of anti-union discrimination . . . [t]he best solution is generally the reinstatement of the worker in his post with payment of unpaid wages and maintenance of acquired rights."[232] Further:

> The Committee considers that legislation which allows the employer in practice to terminate the employment of a worker on condition that he pay the compensation provided for by law in all cases of unjustified dismissal, when the real motive is his trade union membership or activity, is inadequate under the terms of Article 1 of the Convention [ILO Convention concerning the Right to Organise and Collective Bargaining], the most appropriate measure being reinstatement. . . . Where reinstatement is impossible, compensation for anti-union dismissal should be higher than that prescribed for other kinds of dismissal.[233]

Freedom of Association under Domestic Law

In Ecuador, workers have two primary options for exercising their right to organize: unions and *comités de empresa* or company committees. Formation of either requires a minimum of thirty workers—raised in 1991 from the previous

---

organizations against ILO member states alleging violation of the right to freedom of association, makes determinations based on the facts and applicable legal standards, and recommends measures to resolve the disputes.

[231] ILO Committee on Freedom of Association, *Need for rapid and effective protection (Protection against anti-union discrimination)*, Digest of Decisions, Doc. 1204, 1996, para. 737.

[232] International Labour Conference, *1994, Freedom of association and collective bargaining: Protection against acts of anti-union discrimination, Report of the Committee of Experts on the Application of Conventions and Recommendations*, 81st Session, Geneva, 1994, Report III (Part 4B), para. 219. The ILO Committee of Experts is composed of a group of independent experts that reviews reports submitted by ILO member states on their ratification of and compliance with ILO conventions and recommendations. Once a year the committee produces one report on its general observations concerning certain countries and another on a particular theme covered by ILO conventions and recommendations.

[233] Ibid., paras. 220, 221.

minimum of fifteen.[234] Formation of a company committee also requires participation of over 50 percent of the workforce.[235] Company committees and unions fill similar roles, yet only a company committee can negotiate a collective contract. If no such committee exists in a workplace, however, a union may negotiate the contract if over 50 percent of company workers are union members.[236]

According to the ILO Committee of Experts, fixing a minimum number of members for the establishment of a workers' organization does not in itself violate workers' right to organize, but "the number should be fixed in a reasonable manner so that the establishment of organizations is not hindered."[237] In the case of Ecuador, the ILO has explicitly criticized the thirty-worker minimum for unions and company committees, finding:

> Even though the minimum number of 30 workers would be acceptable in the case of sectoral trade unions, the Committee considers that the minimum number should be reduced in the case of [company committees and company unions] so as not to hinder the establishment of such bodies, particularly when it is taken into account that the country has a very large proportion of small enterprises and that the trade union structure is based on enterprise unions.[238]

The ILO has twice recommended that Ecuador "take measures to amend the legislation so as to reduce the minimum number of workers required under the Act (presently 30) in order to establish enterprise unions."[239]

---

[234] Labor Code, Articles 450, 459.

[235] Ibid., Article 459.

[236] Ibid., Article 226.

[237] International Labour Conference, *1994, Freedom of association and collective bargaining: Right of workers and employers to establish and join organizations, Report of the Committee of Experts on the Application of Conventions and Recommendations*, 81st Session, Geneva, 1994, Report III (Part 4B), para. 81.

[238] ILO, *Complaints against the Government of Ecuador presented by the Confederation of Workers of Ecuador (CTE), the Ecuadorian Confederation of Free Trade Union Organisations (CEOSL) and the Latin American Central of Workers (CLAT)*, Report No. 284, Case No. 1617, Vol. LXXV, 1992, Series B, No.3, para. 1006, citing International Labour Conference, *Report of the Committee of Experts on the Application of Conventions and Recommendations*, 79th Session, Geneva, 1992, Report III (Part 4A), pp. 212, 213, 268.

[239] ILO, *Complaint against the Government of Ecuador presented by the Ecuadorian Federation of Agricultural, Agro-Industrial and Food Workers (FETAL)*, Report No. 294,

Ecuador has responded to the complaints filed against it before the ILO by denying that the thirty-worker minimum hinders workers' rights to unionize. The government stated, "[I]t became indispensable and urgent to adjust the rules in the labour law concerning the minimum number of workers necessary for the exercise of the right of association and unionisation, at a time when the country is moving ever faster in a subregional process of economic, customs and industrial integration.... The amendment ... is far from impeding the right of unionisation."[240] When Human Rights Watch asked the undersecretary of labor and human resources (undersecretary of labor) for the coastal and Galápagos region to comment on the change from a fifteen- to thirty-worker minimum, however, he explained:

> When unionizing began, it began because of ideas of the extreme left.... It was so easy to unionize. There was great bitterness among business. The following problem was occurring: ... to avoid leftist unionization, [companies] did not grow sufficiently. They reached twelve or thirteen [workers] in order not to have unions. The same occurs [now at] twenty-nine.[241]

He concluded, therefore, that the difference now is that avoidance of unionization can be accomplished concurrently with reasonable business growth.

Nonetheless, the Constitution states that "workers' right to organization will be guaranteed."[242] Incorporating the language of the ILO Convention concerning Freedom of Association and Protection of the Right to Organise, the Labor Code establishes that "workers ... without distinction and without need for prior authorization, have the right to form professional associations or unions" and, similarly, that "all workers of the [company] will have the right to form part of the company committee, without any distinction."[243] Under the Labor Code, employers are required to "respect all workers' associations" and

---

Case No. 1746, Vol. LXXVII, 1994, Series B, No. 2; ILO, *Complaints against the Government of Ecuador presented by CTE, CEOSL and CLAT* ... , para. 1006

[240] ILO, *Complaints against the Government of Ecuador presented by CTE, CEOSL and CLAT* ... , para. 1001.

[241] Human Rights Watch interview, Alberto Montalvo, undersecretary of labor for the coastal and Galápagos region, Ministry of Labor, Guayaquil, May 16, 2001.

[242] Constitution, Article 35(9).

[243] Labor Code, Articles 447, 467; see Convention concerning the Right to Organise and Collective Bargaining, Article 2.

are prohibited from "interfering with or violating the right to free development of union . . . activities."[244] Despite the general language safeguarding workers' right to freedom of association, a number of crucial weaknesses in Ecuador's labor regime, including the thirty-worker minimum for workers' organizations, render these protections, in practice, virtually meaningless for banana workers and facilitate anti-union discrimination in the sector.

Employers who engage in anti-union discrimination face few, if any, significant repercussions. If an employer violates a worker's right to form a union or company committee, fails to respect a workers' organization, or interferes with a worker's right to develop a workers' association but does not fire the worker for engaging in organizing activity, the employer's conduct can only be sanctioned with a fine of up to U.S. $200 if imposed by the regional Labor Directorate and up to U.S. $50 if imposed by labor inspectors or labor courts.[245] Furthermore, only if Labor Code prohibitions of such conduct are liberally construed, is anti-union discrimination in hiring prohibited under Ecuadorian law. The ILO, however, has clearly stated that anti-union hiring discrimination violates worker' right to organize. As discussed, the ILO Committee on Freedom of Association has found that the international law requirement that workers enjoy "adequate protection against acts of anti-union discrimination in respect of their employment" includes protection against anti-union discrimination in hiring.

If an employer dismisses a worker for union activity, the Labor Code does not require that the worker be reinstated. Instead, the law establishes a list of causes for which a worker can legally be terminated and requires that any worker fired for a reason not enumerated therein receive three months' pay if she has worked three years or less for the same employer and one month's pay for every year worked thereafter.[246] As union activity is not on the list of permissible causes for dismissal, an anti-union dismissal must be compensated with that same fine. The ILO, however, has explicitly found such a sanctions regime to be inadequate to protect freedom of association. As explained above, the ILO Committee of Experts has found imposition of a fine "provided for by law in all cases of unjustified dismissal, when the real motive is . . . trade union membership or activity" to be inadequate under international law.

---

[244] Labor Code, Articles 42(10), 44(j).

[245] Ibid., Article 626. The IMF has also noted that in Ecuador, "the punishment for noncompliance with labor legislation is relatively low." IMF, "Ecuador: Selected Issues and Statistical Annex" . . . , p. 57.

[246] Labor Code, Article 188.

Furthermore, with an estimated average monthly salary of between U.S. $110 and U.S. $150 for adult banana workers, a company's cost-benefit analysis may well militate in favor of dismissing possible union supporters and paying the minimal fine—often less than U.S. $400—as a cost of business and a small price to pay for a union-free workplace.[247] These minimal penalties and those, described above, established for other anti-union employer conduct fall short of those recommended by international legal bodies and fail to deter employers from retaliating against workers who exercise the right to organize.

In addition, ambiguous Labor Code provisions governing employment contracts and inadequate labor law enforcement allow for the use of consecutive short-term contracts and multiple "project contracts" to hire workers year-round to perform everyday tasks on plantations. Such ambiguity and weak enforcement encourage the creation of a vulnerable and precarious "permanent temporary" workforce, excluded from important Labor Code protections governing freedom of association. Plantations also make prolific use of subcontracted temporary labor, frequently in work teams with fewer than the thirty workers required for organization, thus erecting often prohibitive obstacles to workers' exercise of their right to freedom of association.

Together, these factors have largely stifled organization of banana workers in Ecuador and rendered the constitutionally and internationally protected right to organize a fiction for most in the sector. Ecuador has therefore failed to fulfill its obligation under international law "to ensure to all individuals within its territory and subject to its jurisdiction" the right to organize and "to take the necessary steps . . . to adopt such legislative or other measures as may be necessary to give effect" to that right.[248]

"Permanent temporary" workers

The Labor Code allows employers to hire temporary workers to satisfy exigent circumstances, such as temporary personnel reductions, or when the demand for regularly provided products or services increases.[249] In the former

---

[247] Ibid., Articles 459, 462. The indemnity for dismissing a union organizer is only greater if the dismissed worker is a member of a union's elected leadership or if the workers at her workplace have just organized and notified the Labor Inspector but not yet selected union leadership. In such cases, the worker enjoys special union protection, *fuero sindical*, and the fine due is one year's salary, averaging roughly U.S. $1,300 for banana workers. However, reinstatement is still not required. Ibid., Article 187.

[248] ICCPR, Article 2.

[249] Labor Code, Article 17. The Labor Code also permits the use of temporary contracts, not to exceed thirty days, for workers hired to attend to emergencies or extraordinary business needs that, unlike the everyday processing or field activities of banana workers,

case, the contract must state the reason for hiring, the names of the replaced personnel, and the contract's duration; in the latter case, "the contract cannot have a duration of more than 180 consecutive days."[250] The rationale behind this provision is that a worker who provides everyday services to a company on a regular basis, month after month, should be considered a permanent employee and enjoy the corresponding legal protections and benefits.

Nonetheless, this intent can be easily flouted by employers, without contravening the letter of the law, through the use of multiple temporary contracts to satisfy alleged demand increases. Although the Labor Code establishes a cap of 180 consecutive days for one such contract, it does not prohibit the use of consecutive, short-term temporary contracts—weekly or even daily contracts—for many months or years on end, periods that come to far more than 180 consecutive days. In addition, though implicit in the 180-consecutive-day cap for a single contract is a corresponding 180-consecutive-day cap on an employer's right to claim legally an increase in demand, no such limitation is explicitly set forth in the Labor Code. Instead, the proposition that an increase in demand must be transitory can only be inferred. Furthermore, as Minister of Labor Insua explained to Human Rights Watch, "When the temporary contract was created, there was a trick. It said that temporary workers are for when personnel are missing but also when [there is a need for] more workers, and with the [latter], temporary workers were hired all over and the concept of temporary workers was ruined."[251] As the undersecretary of labor for the coastal and Galápagos region observed, it is very difficult to prove that demand has not increased.[252] Thus, by invoking the inherently ambiguous "increase in demand" provision and stringing together a series of short-term contracts, employers create "permanent temporary" employment relationships.

In contrast to temporary contracts, project contracts—contracts for a set amount of work to be performed in a fixed time period—if made for the performance of regular workplace activities, must last, at a minimum, for one year.[253] Only if the project contracts are executed for the performance of tasks

---

are *not* linked to the normal activity of the employers. Seasonal contracts may also be used to hire workers for cyclical labor and are understood to create the right for such workers to be hired back the following cycle or season. As banana production in Ecuador is not cyclical and, instead, involves the performance of all phases of production activity year-round, seasonal contracts are generally not used in the sector. Ibid.

[250] Ibid.

[251] Human Rights Watch interview, Minister of Labor Martín Insua.

[252] Human Rights Watch interview, Undersecretary of Labor Alberto Montalvo.

[253] Labor Code, Articles 14, 16.

outside the scope of normal business operations may they have durations of under one year. Nonetheless, weak enforcement of this requirement gives employers another means by which to employ the same banana workers temporarily, for many months or years on end, to perform everyday tasks, such as processing bananas for shipment.

Using these contracting methods, employers create "permanent temporary" workforces, not covered by Labor Code provisions applicable to legally permanent workers. These contracts—often for a few days or weeks—are rarely put in writing, however, and workers do not know how their employment relationships are classified by the Labor Code. They are aware only that, in the eyes of the law, they are not permanent workers.[254]

The general manager of Bandecua, Del Monte's subsidiary in Ecuador, described the "permanent temporary" worker phenomenon as follows: "Many independent producers have an informal labor system. . . . Workers can arrive for the day, leave, arrive the next day, and the next. . . . [It's] that way all year, and [it] can be that way for years."[255] Gema Caranza, a banana worker employed as a temporary worker for a year and a half on plantations Recreo #1 and #3 in the canton of Naranjal and a year on another group of plantations owned by Arturo Quirola also in Naranjal,[256] explained, "Most of us are temporary. . . . We do not have written contracts. No indefinite contract. That's not custom."[257] Another temporary packing-plant worker, employed on plantation Italia in the canton of Balao, noted that even field workers working for five years are classified as temporary.[258] He said, "In the fields, they work

---

[254] The Labor Code requires that temporary contracts and project contracts for ordinary business activities, with a mandatory minimum duration of one year, be executed in writing. Ibid., Article 19.

[255] Human Rights Watch interview, Marco García.

[256] Gema Caranza told Human Rights Watch that Recreo #1 and #3 primarily produce for Noboa. According to Caranza, Arturo Quirola's plantations are owned by Quirola, a smaller Ecuadorian banana company. Human Rights Watch interview, Gema Caranza, Guayaquil, May 10, 2001.

[257] Ibid.

[258] According to many workers, Italia primarily produces for Dole. Nonetheless, one child, Ricardo Leiva, and two adults, Carla Villa and Antonio Romero, reported occasionally seeing Del Monte stickers on the bananas produced by Italia; one child, Violeta Chamorro, and Villa and Romero stated that they also saw stickers with Noboa's brand name, Bonita, on the plantation's bananas; Romero claimed also to have seen Favorita stickers on the bananas; and Villa asserted that she occasionally saw Chiquita stickers on the fruit. Human Rights Watch interview, Ricardo Leiva, May 19, 2001; Human Rights Watch interview, Violeta Chamorro; Human Rights Watch interview, Carla Chamorro; Human Rights Watch interview, Carla Villa, Naranjal, May 20, 2001;

every day, [but] they are not stable." He continued, explaining that in the packing plants there are workers who work directly for the plant administrator, five or six days a week, year-round, and who are also considered temporary workers. Confused, he said, "We don't understand why they are not permanent."[259] Two other workers employed on plantation Italia estimated that between 40 and 50 percent of the workers on the plantation are temporary workers.[260] The preference for temporary workers, according to Julio Gutiérrez, a retired banana worker, is also evident in the collective bargaining agreement reached between workers on Balao Chico and management, which "before . . . said that if [the company] fired a permanent worker, the company had to replace him with a permanent worker. Now it does not say it." Gutiérrez added, "In Balao Chico, there are workers with over six or eight years. They are permanent, but they are not treated as permanent."[261]

Without permanent contracts, "permanent temporary" workers do not enjoy benefits such as weekends off or paid vacation days.[262] In practice, they are also, in most cases, not affiliated with Ecuador's Social Security Institute, providing public health insurance, despite the Labor Code requirement that employers affiliate all workers from their first day of employment.[263] Julio Gutiérrez explained, "The temporary workers enter with the permanent workers. They work every day, [but] they don't receive benefits."[264] A nurse employed Monday through Friday from 7:00 a.m. to 4:00 p.m. on a plantation primarily

---

Human Rights Watch interview, Antonio Romero; Human Rights Watch interview, Julio Gutiérrez, Naranjal, May 26, 2001. Chiquita, however, denied that it purchased bananas from Italia from 1995 through the end of June 2001, years that encompass the period during which these workers labored on plantation Italia. Letter from Jeffrey Zalla to Human Rights Watch, August 28, 2001.

[259] Human Rights Watch interview, Antonio Romero.

[260] Human Rights Watch interview, Carla Villa; Human Rights Watch interview, Julia Villanueva, Naranjal, May 20, 2001.

[261] Human Rights Watch interview, Julio Gutiérrez, Guayaquil, May, 10, 2001.

[262] The Labor Code grants each worker the right to fifteen uninterrupted paid vacation days annually, including weekends and, after working for over five years for the same employer, one additional vacation day for each year worked, not to exceed fifteen. Labor Code, Article 69. The Labor Code also provides that Saturdays and Sundays are obligatory days of rest, unless circumstances dictate that work cannot be interrupted on those days, in which case, two other days will be designated as days of rest. Ibid., Articles 51-53. Without a stable contract and continuous employment with the same employer, however, these benefits are inaccessible to workers.

[263] Ibid., Article 42(31).

[264] Human Rights Watch interview, Julio Gutiérrez, Guayaquil, May 10, 2001.

producing for Dole, which she asked Human Rights Watch not to identify for fear of repercussions, explained, "I'm a temporary worker by contract. . . . The contract says that I do not have a right to vacations, to a raise, to overtime, for being temporary."[265] A nurse and the head of a pesticide storage facility, working for six days a week for over ten years on another plantation in the canton of Naranjal, remarked that they were also considered temporary workers, did not receive holidays, had no written contracts, and "worked for the company without any benefits." They estimated that of the approximately 300 workers on the plantation, only about twenty are permanent.[266]

Not only do these "permanent temporary" workers not enjoy benefits due to permanent workers, but they enjoy no job security. Because they are not permanent, they have no legal, contractual expectation that their jobs will extend beyond the days or weeks for which they are officially hired, even though they may work on a daily or weekly basis for many months or even years on end. If such a temporary worker, at the expiration of her short-term contract, is suddenly told not to return to work the following day or week, she has not, technically, been fired, simply not rehired. Therefore, the employer is not bound by Labor Code provisions that govern worker dismissal, including those setting forth a finite number of causes for which a worker can legally be dismissed and requiring that the employer pay indemnity to any worker dismissed for a cause not articulated therein.[267] Furthermore, as the Labor Code does not explicitly prohibit anti-union discrimination in hiring, the employer also may not run afoul of Ecuadorian law by failing to rehire a worker for organizing. If, instead, the worker is fired prior to expiration of her short-term contract and the reason for termination is not among the causes for which a worker can be legally dismissed, the worker is due 50 percent of the wages owed for the time remaining on the contract.[268] In the case of a banana worker hired for a month, this will likely amount to a sum of less than U.S. $50; for a worker hired for a five-day week, less than U.S. $15; and for a worker hired for a day, less than U.S. $2. The temporary nurse employed on a plantation primarily producing for Dole added, "The temporary workers do not have the same rights as the permanent workers. The administrator [of the plantation] says that the

---

[265] Human Rights Watch interview, Julia Villanueva. As previously stated, all workers' names have been changed to protect them from potential reprisals.

[266] Human Rights Watch interview, Manuel Vega and Cristina Gallo, Naranjal, May 26, 2001.

[267] Labor Code, Articles 169, 172, 180.

[268] Ibid., Article 181.

temporary workers do not have a right to an opinion. . . . Because they are temporary, in any moment he can grab them and fire them."[269]

Even Minister of Labor Insua, responsible for ensuring Labor Code enforcement in Ecuador, was aware of this problem. He commented to Human Rights Watch that, in practice, temporary workers do not enjoy their legally protected right to organize:

> They can fire them because they [temporary workers] do not have a right to stability. They are fired if they try to unionize. . . . They all fire them. There is not a company that would not fire them. The temporary worker that gets involved in [unionizing] already knows that he's out. . . . Temporary workers are [hired] so as not to have problems with unions. In the moment that the temporary workers unionize, they are fired.[270]

Gema Caranza, after working as a "temporary" worker for a year and a half on Recreo #1 and #3 in the canton of Naranjal, was indefinitely "suspended" on May 7, 2001, allegedly for involvement in union activity. She explained that she was told by the boss of the packing plants that "by order of the administrator of all the plantations of Enrique López," she would be suspended. "[The boss said,] 'He [the administrator] has found out what you're involved in and [is afraid] that you will want to speak with the people and organize.'"[271] According to Caranza, her boss, with whom she had a good working relationship, added, "I told you not to get involved in that—that you'd lose your job." Caranza said that in June 2000, she began to attend union-sponsored events and seminars. In most cases, she said, she invented excuses for her absence, afraid to disclose their true purpose. Before leaving for her first union-sponsored event outside Ecuador, however, she showed her boss the event invitation. She said, "He told me to be careful [and] that others might soon know [what I was doing]." Caranza said, "I knew that if they [the administrator, the plantation owner, or others in management] found out, they would fire me. . . . Because that's the way it is. If they find out, they fire you. This is why most people are scared."[272]

The practical reality for temporary workers is, therefore, that their right to freedom of association is effectively nullified. In fact, even key Labor Ministry officials do not know the right exists. Although Minister of Labor Insua

---

[269] Human Rights Watch interview, Julia Villanueva.

[270] Human Rights Watch interview, Minister of Labor Martín Insua.

[271] Human Rights Watch telephone interview, Gema Caranza, Naranjal, June 8, 2001.

[272] Ibid.; Human Rights Watch interview, Gema Caranza, Guayaquil, May 10, 2001.

acknowledged temporary workers' right to organize, high-ranking officials of the Undersecretariat of Labor and Human Resources (Undersecretariat of Labor) for the Coastal and Galápagos Region—directly responsible for approving and registering unions as well as enforcing labor law in that region—believe that their right to organize is not even guaranteed by Ecuadorian law. Despite the Labor Code's explicit protection of the right of "workers . . . *without distinction*" to organize, the undersecretary of labor for the coastal and Galápagos region, who heads the regional undersecretariat, told Human Rights Watch:

> Temporary workers are precarious. They do not have the same guarantees as permanent workers because they do not have the right to indemnity. . . . They do not have the right to unionize. . . . [Unions] could not count temporary workers to meet the minimum number of workers [required for union formation].[273]

A representative of the undersecretariat's Legal Department similarly stated, "Temporary workers who work per month do not have the right to organize because they are not stable. . . . If there are temporary workers in the statutes [or] founding papers, they do not count towards the minimum [number required to unionize]."[274] And the head of the undersecretariat's Labor Directorate, who oversees the regional labor inspectors and registers unions for the undersecretariat, told Human Rights Watch, "Only stable workers [can unionize]. . . . Temporary workers . . . cannot affiliate. . . . They cannot affiliate after [union formation, either]."[275]

According to Minister of Labor Insua, however, the difficulty temporary workers face in exercising their right to freedom of association is not as prejudicial to their interests as it might at first seem because "labor law says that the collective contract cannot exclude anyone. . . . [It's] for everyone."[276] The Supreme Court of Ecuador has, in fact, found that "the collective labor contract protects all workers subject to the Labor Code's regime, even though they were not affiliated to the association of workers that signed it."[277]

---

[273] Human Rights Watch interview, Undersecretary of Labor Alberto Montalvo.

[274] Human Rights Watch interview, Mauro Vargas, Department of Legal Assistance, Undersecretary of Labor for the Coastal and Galápagos Region, Guayaquil, May 16, 2001.

[275] Human Rights Watch interview, Efraín Duque.

[276] Human Rights Watch interview, Minister of Labor Martín Insua.

[277] Resolution of the Supreme Court of Justice, March 8, 1990, cited in Labor Code, Article 224.

Therefore, though temporary workers might not be union or company committee members, they legally should enjoy the benefits of any negotiated collective agreement in their workplaces. This does not occur in practice, however, according to a labor leader and several workers who spoke with Human Rights Watch.

An Ecuadorian labor leader representing the AFL-CIO's Solidarity Center in Ecuador explained that, in practice, if temporary workers are to be covered by a collective agreement, the union or company committee that is party to the agreement must negotiate a specific provision that explicitly extends coverage to the temporary workers.[278] For example, Carla Villa, a worker employed on plantation Italia, explained, "Those who are not members of the committee do not receive the benefits of the collective agreement."[279] Her coworker elaborated, stating that there are roughly ninety workers on the company committee, that they are all permanent workers, and that, as a temporary worker, she enjoyed "no benefits of the collective agreement. [They are] only for the committee, who are permanent workers."[280]

Use of subcontractors

Approximately half the adults interviewed by Human Rights Watch and almost all the children identified their bosses not as the plantation administrators but as the leaders of small work teams, either in the fields or the packing plants.[281] These "team leaders," as the workers call them, are responsible for finding, hiring, and overseeing the workers and paying them directly, either in cash or check, often from money given to them by the plantation administrators. According to a banana producer and long-time member of the banana industry in El Oro province, "Normally, they are subcontractors, but semi-permanent subcontractors—months or years on the same plantation."[282] Juan Luis Alfaro, a subcontractor employed for six years by plantation Colón in the canton of Balao,

---

[278] Human Rights Watch interview, Patricio Contreras, Quito, May 22, 2001. The AFL-CIO's Solidarity Center promotes labor rights and labor organizing around the world.

[279] Human Rights Watch interview, Carla Villa.

[280] Human Rights Watch interview, Julia Villanueva.

[281] The workers did not distinguish between team leaders who were permanent employees of the company and team leaders who were contracted by the company to hire subcontracted work teams. Therefore, Human Rights Watch is unable to determine with certainty how many of these workers were, in fact, subcontracted.

[282] Human Rights Watch telephone interview, Arturo Buchelli, general manager, Movilizadora de Banano, S.A. (MOBANSA), Machala, July 7, 2001.

stated that he rotated with his team of sixteen workers among the plantation's three packing plants.

> They made me sign a contract to hire personnel to process bananas in the packing plant. . . . They wanted to charge me taxes. . . . They made me do a payroll. I had to make the rolls [and] put [the workers'] names and sign [the] blank [paper]. They put the amount. They gave me money to pay the team. . . . They gave me cash.[283]

According to the workers who make up these work teams, most of whom work three or four days a week, their team leaders notify them, usually one day prior, when they will be needed on the plantations. A twelve-year-old girl working on the plantation group Las Fincas explained, "They come tell you so you know when they need workers."[284] Lisa Moreno, a thirteen-year-old, described being recruited by team leaders, saying, "The boss came looking for me at home because they needed people on Colón. Recently, two weeks ago . . . the [team] boss of Pachina came looking."[285] Victor Garza, a sixty-two-year-old worker, explained that he had worked for contractors for approximately forty years. He stated that since 1998, he had worked in Balao on plantations San Vicente, Luz Belén, and San José, owned by Parazul, S.A., for subcontractors hired by the plantations' administrators.[286] He told Human Rights Watch, "I am not a permanent worker. . . . No written contract, verbal. They come in trucks to pick us up. They communicate to you so that later, the next day, they pick you up."[287]

Francisco Lazo, a management-side lawyer in private practice in Ecuador, told Human Rights Watch that subcontracting "is how to break unionization. It is used a lot in the banana sector."[288] Exactly how widespread the use of subcontractors is in the sector, however, is difficult to estimate. Use varies

---

[283] Human Rights Watch interview, Juan Luis Alfaro.

[284] Human Rights Watch interview, Fabiola Cardozo.

[285] Human Rights Watch interview, Lisa Moreno.

[286] Victor Garza stated that both Luz Belén and San Vicente primarily produce for Dole. Garza added, however, that, on occasion, he had seen boxes produced on Luz Belén for Noboa. Another banana worker working on Luz Belén, Arturo Zedillo, also stated that the plantation produces primarily for Dole. Human Rights Watch interview, Victor Garza; Human Rights Watch interview, Arturo Zedillo, Balao, May 27, 2001.

[287] Human Rights Watch interview, Victor Garza.

[288] Human Rights Watch interview, Francisco Lazo, attorney, Quito, May 8, 2001.

greatly from plantation to plantation and company to company. For example, the executive vice president of Favorita, the second-largest nationally owned banana company in Ecuador, told Human Rights Watch that on the plantations of Reybancorp, its banana-producing subsidiary, only 700 of the 5,600 workers—13 percent—are direct company employees; the other 87 percent work for subcontractors.[289] In contrast, Noboa, the largest nationally owned banana company, stated that on its plantations, it directly employs approximately 5,300 workers and does not use subcontractors.[290]

Like temporary workers employed directly by plantation administrators, subcontracted workers, also working on a temporary weekly or daily basis and often without a written contract, lack job security. Cecilia Menéndez, a worker formerly employed on plantation Colón, explained to Human Rights Watch that after she complained about her salary, she knew she had been suspended because, "He [my team leader] stopped looking for me. . . . If he advises me that I should go to work, I go. If not, not." Menéndez added that she learned a lesson from her experience: "You should never complain because it doesn't matter to them. Better to keep quiet."[291]

In addition, though subcontracted workers perform labor from which the company, not the individual subcontractor, directly benefits and may receive wages indirectly from the company, the workers are legally employed only by the subcontractor. This contradicts the spirit of the Constitution, which provides that, "without prejudice to the principal responsibility of the [direct contractor], . . . the person for whose benefit work is realized or services are given will be jointly responsible for compliance with labor obligations, even though the contract is executed by an intermediary."[292] Despite the Constitution's inclusive intent, workers are not permitted to organize and then bargain collectively with that "person for whose benefit work is realized or services are given"—that is, the company that, to a great extent, controls their salaries, benefits, and workplace health and safety conditions. Instead, they can only legally organize

---

[289] Human Rights Watch interview, Vicente Wong.

[290] Human Rights Watch interview, Francisco Chávez. Human Rights Watch interviewed four adult workers who worked or had worked on Alamos-Rey Rancho, a plantation directly owned by Noboa, and they all stated that they were direct company employees and that subcontractors were rarely used.

[291] Human Rights Watch interview, Cecilia Menéndez.

[292] Constitution, Article 35(11). Similarly, according to the Labor Code, an employer and that employer's intermediary hired to contract personnel to perform everyday company tasks share "joint responsibility" for the violation of "obligations to the worker." Labor Code, Article 41.

and negotiate collectively with the subcontractor, the most direct source of their salaries and, therefore, their legal employer.

Even if workers determined that it was worthwhile to organize and then negotiate with their subcontractor, however, they would most likely not be able to do so because the Labor Code requires a minimum of thirty workers to form a union or company committee. As subcontracted teams usually consist of fewer than thirty workers, organization is not even an option for most subcontracted workers. For example, none of the twenty-five current and former adult banana workers interviewed by Human Rights Watch reported working in teams with over twenty-eight workers. According to Joaquín Vásquez, president of UROCAL, an association of small producers, the work teams in packing plants usually consist of between fifteen and twenty workers and, in the fields, no more than twenty-five.[293] And not only does the thirty-worker minimum often preclude subcontracted workers from organizing their work teams, it can also preclude organization among workers laboring on plantations where subcontracting is so heavily utilized that the number of direct company employees is reduced to fewer than thirty.

When asked why plantations of Reybancorp, the banana-producing subsidiary of Favorita, rely so heavily on subcontracted workers, the executive vice president of Favorita told Human Rights Watch, "The advantage is flexibility" and "to avoid a high concentration [of workers] on just one worksite with regards to payment. . . . For more reasonable administrative management, so the company does not have to dedicate itself to this [administrative] work."[294] Officials of the Ministry of Labor, however, explained the prolific use of subcontractors differently. The undersecretary of labor for the coastal and Galápagos region stated that companies allow the number of their directly contracted personnel on a given worksite to reach twenty-nine and then "subcontract so as not to have [unions]."[295] A labor inspector for the regional undersecretariat, who had visited banana plantations, added, "On the majority of plantations, there are fewer then thirty [direct employees]. They [the plantations] divide into various companies in order to avoid unionization [or] they subcontract and use third-party companies."[296] Minister of Labor Insua told Human Rights Watch, "Having subcontracted personnel is a way to avoid

---

[293] Human Rights Watch interview, Joaquín Vásquez.

[294] Human Rights Watch interview, Vicente Wong.

[295] Human Rights Watch interview, Undersecretary of Labor Alberto Montalvo.

[296] Human Rights Watch interview, Ricardo Campozano, regional labor inspector for the coastal and Galápagos region, Ministry of Labor, Guayaquil, May 16, 2001.

unionization and not comply with labor laws."²⁹⁷ At the International Labour Conference in Geneva in June 2001, the minister publicly criticized "'subcontracting' . . . in his country that permits many national and foreign companies to function without one directly employed worker" and indicated that among the primary reasons companies adopt this practice of contracting is "to get rid of unions."²⁹⁸

Weak protections for permanent workers

Even those workers lucky enough to have been hired with permanent employment contracts directly by plantation owners risk dismissal if they attempt to organize. As discussed above, the Labor Code does not require reinstatement when a worker is fired for engaging in union activity, and, instead, in most cases, only requires the payment of a relatively small fine.²⁹⁹ As Undersecretary of Labor Montalvo noted, "If the dismissal is for disharmony, [the fines] will not be an obstacle. . . . It does not function to dissuade. If [the employer] wants to fire [the worker], it will fire [him]."³⁰⁰ Francisco Lazo, a business-side labor lawyer, told Human Rights Watch:

> Companies . . . try to avoid unionization because it implies they have to negotiate a collective contract and increase production costs. . . . When the conditions are very bad, they resort to firing. Before, there was [some] minimal stability. The company had to recognize two [years' pay for indemnity]. The *visto bueno* [mandatory approval for dismissal from the Labor Inspectorate] was more complicated. . . . Now, three months is the indemnity for illegal firing. . . . It's harder for the workers and more favorable for the employer. It's easier to fire workers.³⁰¹

Minister Insua also explained, "If the possibility of people wanting to unionize is seen, they are all fired. . . . They prefer to bring workers from other areas than to have a union. They fire them and they propose a diminished indemnity, and if they don't accept it, they can go to court. For the field worker,

---

²⁹⁷ Human Rights Watch interview, Minister of Labor Martín Insua.

²⁹⁸ "Ministro Insua denunció abuso subcontratción" ["Minister Insua denounces the abuse of subcontracting"], *El Universo*, June 20, 2001.

²⁹⁹ Labor Code, Article 188.

³⁰⁰ Human Rights Watch interview, Undersecretary of Labor Alberto Montalvo.

³⁰¹ Human Rights Watch interview, Francisco Lazo.

Freedom of Association 77

... it's too difficult [to go to court]. ... The judicial avenue is very long—two years at a minimum."[302] The attorney Lazo concurred, noting:

> I can fire workers if I want. I don't necessarily have to pay. It is the worker who has to complain to the Ministry of Labor. The worker is obligated to file the case. The case can last ... two years. Companies that tell a man to leave tell him that they will not pay and don't pay. A company can pay much more and [get] good lawyers so [the case] lasts many years. ... They prefer to pay the lawyer [than the worker].[303]

Commenting on the anti-union climate in the banana sector, the general manager of Del Monte's Ecuadorian subsidiary noted:

> The [Ecuadorian] banana producer is very radical. He has a phobia of unions. ... They cut at the roots any efforts [to organize]. They fire the people. ... In meetings of producers, I've heard that they will do anything not to have unions. ... The producers here see Costa Rica, Guatemala, and Colombia and talk with producers from those countries who are tied by the unions. They don't want ... that problem.[304]

Similarly, a labor inspector for the Undersecretariat of Labor for the Coastal and Galápagos Region told Human Rights Watch, "There have been cases in which they [workers] have wanted to form unions or company committees, and they

---

[302] Human Rights Watch interview, Minister of Labor Martín Insua.

[303] Human Rights Watch interview, Francisco Lazo.

[304] Human Rights Watch interview, Marco García. Nevertheless, the International Confederation of Free Trade Unions (ICFTU) notes that more trade unionists—135—were killed in Colombia in 2000 than in any other country. ICFTU, *Annual Survey of Violations of Trade Union Rights 2001* (Brussels, Belgium: ICFTU, 2000), pp. 5, 44, 53.

have been fired. In the banana sector, this is an everyday occurrence."[305] The director of the undersecretariat's Labor Directorate added, "Employers are afraid of workers' organizations. If they discover them, they [the workers] are fired . . . before notifying here [to register the organization]."[306]

---

[305] Human Rights Watch interview, Ricardo Campozano.

[306] Human Rights Watch interview, Efraín Duque.

VI. BANANA-EXPORTING CORPORATIONS

At the World Economic Forum, Davos, on 31 January 1999, UN Secretary-General Kofi A. Annan challenged world business leaders to "embrace and enact" the Global Compact, both in their individual corporate practices and by supporting appropriate public policies. The Secretary-General asked world business to uphold:

> *Principle 3: freedom of association and the effective recognition of the right to collective bargaining; . . .*
> *Principle 5: the effective abolition of child labour.*

—United Nations Global Compact.[307]

International law establishes labor rights and standards that states are required to uphold. If states fulfilled this obligation, they would demand that corporations also respect these rights and standards. Corporations, however, are not directly regulated by international law. Nonetheless, as reflected in the United Nations Global Compact, cited above, there is an international consensus that corporations have a duty to uphold workers' rights. There is also an emerging consensus, evidenced in various corporate codes of conduct, that corporations have a responsibility to take steps to ensure that labor rights are respected not only in their directly owned corporate facilities but throughout their supply chains as well.

When countries, like Ecuador, do not adequately enforce labor laws or lack sufficient legal protections to guarantee workers' rights, the government fails to fulfill its duty to protect labor rights. These governmental acts of omission enable employers to commit labor rights violations with impunity and thereby allow them to benefit from workers' rights abuses. Exporter corporations may enter into direct contractual relationships with these employers in whose

---

[307] United Nations. (January 31, 1999). *The Global Compact*. [Online]. Available: http://www.unglobalcompact.org/gc/unweb.nsf/content/thenine.htm [August 1, 2001]. The Global Compact is not a regulatory instrument nor a code of conduct. Instead, it identifies nine "universal principles" and asks companies to act on these principles in their own corporate domains, become public advocates for the principles, and participate in the activities of the Global Compact, including thematic dialogues. Participating companies are asked to post, at least once a year, on the Global Compact website concrete steps they have taken to act on any of the nine principles and the lessons they learned from doing so. United Nations General Secretary's Office. (January 17, 2001). *The Global Compact: What it is.* [Online]. Available: http://www.unglobalcompact.org/gc/unweb.nsf/content/whatitis.htm [August 23, 2001].

workplaces workers' rights are violated to purchase product for export. When those financial or contractual relationships are forged and the exporting corporations fail to use their influence to demand respect for labor rights in those workplaces, in some cases contravening their own codes of conduct, the exporting corporations also facilitate and benefit from the labor rights violations because they receive goods produced under abusive conditions. Human Rights Watch believes that, in such cases, the exporting corporations have a fundamental responsibility to ensure respect for labor rights in the workplaces of their suppliers and are complicit in the workers' rights violations when they fail to do so. And when the exporting corporations sanction for use on their third-party supplier plantations pesticides that may be toxic for children, Human Rights Watch considers the corporations to be highly complicit in the human rights violations suffered by the child workers exposed to those chemicals while laboring on the supplier plantations.

As discussed below, Human Rights Watch believes that Dole and Noboa have failed to ensure respect for workers' rights by primary suppliers, from which they purchase regularly, and that Chiquita, Del Monte, and Favorita, as well as Dole and Noboa, have failed to do so on plantations from which they purchase occasionally. These exporting corporations have therefore benefited from and, Human Rights Watch believes, are complicit in labor rights abuses on these supplier plantations. In the cases of Chiquita and Dole, they have also disregarded their own policies that recognize corporate responsibility for labor conditions on supplier plantations—policies established through Dole's "signatory membership" in Social Accountability 8000 (SA8000), "a global humane workplace standard" for "company-owned and *supplier facilities*" [emphasis added],[308] and in Chiquita's internal code of conduct, based largely on SA8000.

Because of heavy corporate reliance on third-party suppliers and because the vast majority of workers interviewed by Human Rights Watch labored on supplier plantations, when Human Rights Watch met with the Ecuadorian representatives of Noboa, Dole, Favorita, Del Monte, and Chiquita, the five corporations discussed in this investigation, the conversations focused on their policies with respect to labor practices on the plantations from which they purchase bananas—both primary suppliers with which they have long-standing contractual relationships and suppliers from which they purchase only on

---

[308] Social Accountability International (SAI). (No date). *SA8000 Signatory Program*. [Online]. Available: http://www.cepaa.org/membership.htm [January 30, 2002].

occasion.[309] The companies uniformly assumed responsibility for compliance with Ecuadorian law and claimed to monitor labor conditions, including child labor and health and safety, and to allow freedom of association on their directly owned plantations. Nonetheless, although the companies' representatives in Ecuador, to varying degrees, recognized that labor rights violations may occur on their supplier plantations, they all ultimately disclaimed any obligation to mandate respect for workers' rights on those plantations.[310]

For example, the executive president of Favorita, Segundo Wong, wrote to Human Rights Watch that "labor rights of workers hired to perform farm work in Reybanpac or Reybancorp farms are strictly within social and economic legislation in force in Ecuador, including the labor code. In particular, rights related to compensation, social benefits and ages are strictly adhered to and closely monitored by management."[311] The executive vice president of Favorita, Vicente Wong, told Human Rights Watch, however, that, with respect to its supplier producers, "They are the bosses of their own plantations. . . . We cannot interfere in their administration process. . . . It is private land and property of the administrators."[312]

Similarly, the head of human resources at Noboa, Francisco Chávez, stated, "The law only obligates the employers with dependent relationships. The producers are governed by the laws, but it is not for us to make them comply with that. We don't have anything to do with that. . . . We don't intervene in that part. It's not in the contract." Chávez continued, "We demand that they comply with quality norms. If not, we don't buy from them. There are quality . . . inspectors who go to these plantations . . . [to verify] quality norms and the process. Nothing with labor. We cannot intervene because they are private properties."[313]

The general manager of Bandecua, Del Monte's Ecuadorian subsidiary, expressed a similar attitude towards suppliers, stating, "They don't have to comply with any rules of Del Monte with the exception of quality of fruit and

---

[309] With the exception of four adult workers laboring on Alamos-Rey Rancho, owned directly by Noboa, the workers interviewed by Human Rights Watch were not employed on plantations directly owned by any of these five corporations.

[310] Human Rights Watch telephone interview, José Anchundia; Human Rights Watch interview, Francisco Chávez; Human Rights Watch interview, Ricardo Flores; Human Rights Watch interview, Marco García; Human Rights Watch interview, Vicente Wong.

[311] Letter from Dr. Segundo Wong to Human Rights Watch, July 17, 2001.

[312] Human Rights Watch interview, Vicente Wong.

[313] Human Rights Watch interview, Francisco Chávez.

technical procedures, [i.e.], . . . chemical products. With respect to workers, nothing. Health and safety, nothing. . . . We don't have any rules regarding underage workers. It's the decision of each hacienda." He explained that "Del Monte's engineers supervise [the producers]," monitoring the production process and the use of pesticides, "but nothing with regards to personnel. Only with respect to production.[314]

Ricardo Flores, general manager of Brundicorpi, Chiquita's subsidiary in Ecuador, in slight contrast, expressed company concern for the labor practices on supplier plantations, but nonetheless concluded that while Chiquita can make recommendations regarding labor policies, the recommendations are, in the end, unenforceable. For example, he noted that in May 2000, Chiquita adopted a code of conduct, but, he explained, "We are in the process of implementing it internally. Later, we have to convince suppliers that they should comply with the code of conduct, [but] we are not in a position to demand it, only to convince them that it is good. . . . We cannot demand [it] of anyone."[315] Flores explained, "We have people in the fields who visit the plantations to verify the quality of the fruit . . . that the fruit is protected according to standards—level of leaf infection, processing at the correct age, . . . that they are using the approved chemicals. . . . Nothing with respect to the labor question. We don't have any right to do that."[316] Human Rights Watch believes, however, that not only do banana-exporting corporations have the right to monitor compliance with high labor standards on their supplier plantations but the responsibility to do so, using their financial leverage to demand respect for workers' rights.

When Human Rights Watch posed similar questions to representatives of UBESA, the Dole subsidiary in Ecuador, different answers were given by the agricultural engineer, responsible for environmental safety, and the director of human resources, responsible for administering labor policies. The agricultural engineer, Ivan Bermúdez, explained that UBESA provides "guides" to its primary suppliers, which include worker health and safety standards, and that each primary supplier should develop internal regulations based on these guides. According to Bermúdez, UBESA sends personnel from its Department of Environmental Safety to primary supplier plantations to provide technical assistance and oversee compliance with the company's internal guidelines. Bermúdez commented, "We don't limit ourselves to buying fruit." With respect to child labor, Bermúdez told Human Rights Watch, "Our producers . . . are

---

[314] Human Rights Watch interview, Marco García.

[315] Human Rights Watch interview, Ricardo Flores.

[316] Ibid.

conscious that they should not hire [children]. It has happened, and we have indicated that they should not do it, and they do not do it again."[317] He noted, however, that as an agricultural engineer supervising environmental safety, he was not qualified to speak on labor matters, including child labor and worker health and safety, and that Human Rights Watch should contact the director of human resources.

When Human Rights Watch asked UBESA's director of human resources, José Anchundia, about labor conditions, including child labor and health and safety, on the plantations of the company's third-party suppliers, he stated emphatically:

> We do not have jurisdiction over that. They have to follow the law. It is their discretion. Here contracting minors is prohibited, . . . [but] we do not intervene in that. Absolutely not. It's their business. . . . We do not have that responsibility. Nothing to do there. Our contract is limited to quality and technical assistance. . . . We give technical assistance to obtain the optimal quality. We have inspectors to oversee the quality of fruit. . . . The only obligation we have with respect to those plantations is that we buy [bananas] and pay the official price [set by] the government, but the responsibility with regard to contracting personnel and health and safety corresponds to the plantation owner, the owner of the property.[318]

These responses are disappointing. Exporting corporations exercise the power of the purse and could insist that high labor standards be met on their supplier plantations.

Codes of Conduct

As discussed, Ecuadorian representatives from all five exporting companies ultimately renounced any responsibility for labor conditions on the plantations of third-party suppliers. Nevertheless, Dole has publicly pledged to work towards the adoption of a code of conduct that explicitly requires the corporation to accept responsibility, through oversight and monitoring, for labor practices on both its directly-owned plantations and its independent, third-party suppliers. And Chiquita has already adopted such a code. Both Dole's public commitment and Chiquita's code of conduct, however, fail to require immediate respect for workers' rights on the companies' third-party supplier plantations.

---

[317] Human Rights Watch interview, Ivan Bermúdez, agricultural engineer, supervisor of environmental security, UBESA, S.A., Guayaquil, May 17, 2001.

[318] Human Rights Watch telephone interview, José Anchundia.

Therefore, on plantations primarily or occasionally supplying Dole and on plantations occasionally supplying Chiquita where the workers interviewed by Human Rights Watch labored, these public promises have had minimal impact on labor conditions. Similarly, the International Finance Corporation (IFC), a member of the World Bank Group that financed a project for Favorita, has published an "Interim Guidance" to its "Policy Statement on Harmful Child and Forced Labor" that encourages, but does not require, companies that receive IFC financing to review major supplier relationships and ask suppliers to "address" instances of harmful child labor.[319] That policy came into force in March 1998.

Dole

Although UBESA's director of human resources, responsible for the labor policies of Dole's Ecuadorian subsidiary, asserted that the company lacks jurisdiction over labor practices and conditions on its supplier plantations, Dole's web site states, "Dole does not knowingly purchase products from any commercial producers employing minors."[320] In a letter to Human Rights Watch, Dole also stated:

> It is Dole's policy to comply with all applicable regulations and laws of any country in which it or its affiliates operate, including those relating to labor practices. . . . Dole audits its suppliers in a number of areas, including labor rights.[321]

The company, however, would "not comment on monitoring or inspections of a specific producer or plantation."[322]

Since November 1999, Dole has also been a "signatory member" of SA8000.[323] However, unlike SA8000 accredited corporations, which have been certified as complying with all SA8000 requirements, signatory members must

---

[319] IFC. (June 30, 2000). *IFC-Financed Company First Recipient of Environmental Certification.* [Online]. Available: http://wbln0018.worldbank.org/IFCExt/pressroom/ ifcpressroom.nsf [September 10, 2001]; IFC. (March 1998). *Harmful Child Labor: Interim Guidance.* [Online]. Available: http://www.ifc.org/enviro/enviro/childlabor/ child.htm [September 10, 2001].

[320] Dole Food Company, Inc. (No date). *Labor Policies.* [Online]. Available: http://www.dole.com/company/business/lbr.policies.ghtml [June 23, 2001].

[321] Letter from Freya Maneki to Human Rights Watch, October 8, 2001.

[322] Ibid.

[323] Human Rights Watch telephone interview, Matthew Shapiro, marketing director, SAI, New York, NY, July 16, 2001.

only promise to achieve full compliance within an unspecified "reasonable period of time."[324] Thus, as an SA8000 signatory member, Dole pays a $10,000 annual membership fee but is not yet certified as compliant with SA8000 standards.[325]

The SA8000 signatory program, begun in November 1999, describes itself as a tool for companies to "demonstrate a real and credible commitment to achieving decent working conditions *in their supply chains*" [emphasis added].[326] In keeping with this commitment, during the three-year membership period, Dole must: define the scope of its operations that it intends to bring into compliance with SA8000; establish a schedule for facilities to achieve certification and a date for SA8000 to become a requirement for any new suppliers; develop a plan and management system for achieving this goal; and publicly issue an annual progress report, the first of which was due for Dole in December 2001.[327] At the time of signatory membership application, Dole defined its "scope" to include all primary banana-producing facilities, which, according to Matthew Shapiro, marketing director for SA8000, extends to all third-party banana suppliers. Shapiro explained that even those plantations with which Dole does not have long-standing contractual relationships and from which it purchases bananas only sporadically are considered suppliers under SA8000.[328] When Dole applied for signatory membership, it was required to submit a statement formally adopting SA8000 as the code for labor practices on all of its banana supplier plantations and to communicate this policy to those facilities.[329] During the signatory membership period, Dole must notify the suppliers when SA8000 certification will become a contractual obligation and, through assessments and audits, work directly with them to achieve compliance.[330] To achieve SA8000 certification, Dole must:

---

[324] SAI. (No date). *SA8000 Signatory Program.* [Online].

[325] Human Rights Watch telephone interview, Matthew Shapiro, September 6, 2001. According to the SA8000 Signatory Program fee schedule, a member with an annual revenue of between $1 billion and $10 billion, such as Dole, must pay a $10,000 annual fee. SAI. (No date). *Application for SA8000 Signatory Status.* [Online]. Available: http://www.cepaa.org/membership.htm [January 30, 2002], p. 6.

[326] SAI. (No date). *SA8000 Signatory Program.* [Online].

[327] Ibid.; SAI. (No date). *Application for SA8000 Signatory Status.* [Online]; Human Rights Watch telephone interview, Matthew Shapiro, July 16, 2001.

[328] Human Rights Watch telephone interview, Matthew Shapiro, July 16, 2001.

[329] SAI. (No date). *Application for SA8000 Signatory Status.* [Online]. . . . , p. 1.

[330] SAI. (No date). *SA8000 Signatory Program.* [Online]; Human Rights Watch telephone interview, Matthew Shapiro, July 16, 2001.

establish and maintain appropriate procedures to evaluate and select suppliers/subcontractors (and, where appropriate, sub-suppliers) based on their ability to meet the requirements of this standard. . . . The company shall maintain appropriate records of suppliers'/subcontractors' (and, where appropriate, sub-suppliers') commitments to social accountability . . . and reasonable evidence that the requirements of this standard are being met by suppliers and subcontractors.[331]

The "Social Accountability Requirements" established by SA8000 ban companies from hiring children—defined as persons under fifteen, unless local minimum age law stipulates a higher age or the country meets the developing country exception under the ILO Minimum Age Convention, in which case children are defined as persons under fourteen. SA8000 also requires companies to establish procedures to "provide adequate support to enable [the child worker] to attend and remain in school until no longer a child as defined above."[332] SA8000 also establishes that "the company shall not expose children or young workers to situations in or outside of the workplace that are hazardous, unsafe, or unhealthy."[333] In addition to setting forth child labor protections, SA8000 requires:

> That the company shall provide a safe and healthy working environment; . . . That the company shall respect the right of all personnel to form and join trade unions of their choice; . . . That the company shall not allow

---

[331] SAI. (2001). *Social Accountability 8000*. [Online]. Available: http://www.cepaa.org/SA8000%20Standard.htm [January 30, 2001], pp. 7-8. Records of suppliers', subcontractors', and sub-suppliers' commitments to social accountability shall include their written commitments to:

a) conform to all requirements of this standard . . . ;

b) participate in the company's monitoring activities as requested;

c) promptly implement remedial and corrective action to address any nonconformance identified against the requirements of this standard; [and]

d) promptly and completely inform the company of any and all relevant business relationship(s) with other suppliers/subcontractors and sub-suppliers.

Ibid., pp. 7-8, para. 9.7.

[332] Ibid., p. 5, para. 1.2.

[333] Ibid., p. 5, para. 1.4. SA8000 defines "young worker" as any worker over the age of a child and under eighteen. Ibid., p. 5.

behaviour, including gestures, language and physical contact, that is sexually coercive, threatening, abusive or exploitative; . . . That the company shall ensure that labour-only contracting arrangements . . . are not undertaken in an effort to avoid fulfilling its obligations to personnel under applicable laws pertaining to labour and social security legislation and regulations.[334]

Despite Dole's professed commitment to achieve compliance with SA8000 standards, as stated above, of the forty-five children with whom Human Rights Watch spoke, thirty-two stated that, at some time, they had worked on plantations primarily producing for Dole and an additional three on plantations producing sporadically for Dole. The average age at which these children began working on plantations supplying Dole was approximately eleven and a half, with two starting at age eight and two at age nine. Most of the children, as described, labored in conditions that violated their right to health, and the majority no longer attended school. Three of the young girls interviewed also described sexual harassment they had experienced in the packing plants of one of Dole's primary suppliers—the plantation group Las Fincas in Balao. Several adults also told Human Rights Watch about the "permanent temporary" contracting arrangements they had with Dole suppliers or subcontractors hired by those suppliers that impeded their enjoyment of labor rights. Although Human Rights Watch wrote to Dole to confirm the company's contractual relationships with these plantations, Dole asserted that information regarding these relationships is "proprietary business information, which Dole does not publicly disclose."[335]

Despite these labor rights abuses, Dole has not violated the terms of its SA8000 signatory membership because, as a signatory member, Dole has only committed to bring its supplier facilities into full SA8000 compliance within "a reasonable time period." In fact, as Dole highlighted in its letter to Human Rights Watch, the company was "honored with the first-ever ethical workplace award from Social Accountability International."[336] Nevertheless, while Dole

---

[334] Ibid., pp. 5-7.

[335] Letter from Freya Maneki to Human Rights Watch, October 8, 2001.

[336] Ibid. The award was presented to Dole in June 2000 after Dole's Spanish subsidiary, the largest fresh fruit and vegetable producer in Spain, became the first agricultural operation in the world to obtain SA8000 certification. SGS International Certification Services. (June 2000). *Dole Food Company Honored With First-Ever Ethical Workplace Award.* [Online]. Available: http://www.ics.sgsna.com/news/Dole.htm [October 10, 2001].

progressively implements SA8000 standards within a "reasonable" timeframe on its supplier plantations worldwide, workers' rights on its supplier plantations in Ecuador continue to be violated, as domestic labor laws designed to protect those workers remain inadequate or unenforced.[337]

Chiquita

Chiquita has also made several public efforts to demonstrate the company's commitment to workers' rights on its supplier plantations. As explained by the general manager of Chiquita's Ecuadorian subsidiary, Ricardo Flores, Chiquita adopted a code of conduct in May 2000 titled, *Living by our Core Values*. Though Chiquita is not certified by nor a signatory member of SA8000, its code of conduct is only "slightly modified from the current SA8000 standard" and includes all the SA8000 provisions enumerated above, including those governing evaluation, selection, and monitoring of third-party suppliers.[338] The code of conduct already governs all Chiquita's directly owned operations worldwide and, in addition, states that all suppliers will be provided a copy of the code of conduct:

> and we will ask them to adhere to the standards of conduct we demonstrate in our owned operations. . . . [W]e will establish a program to work with our principal suppliers . . . to assess their current Social Responsibility performance and to establish plans to meet these standards within a reasonable period of time.[339]

Similarly, in its *2000 Corporate Responsibility Report*, Chiquita asserts, "We are committed to achieving the same quality standards, including standards for social and environmental responsibility, on all bananas marketed by Chiquita, whether we produce them on our own farms or purchase them from independent growers." According to the report, Chiquita "[u]ltimately . . . will decide whether to initiate or renew contracts with growers based not only on

---

[337] Stanflico, a banana growing and packing division of Dole Philippines, Inc., has been certified SA8000 compliant. SAI. (August 2001). *SA8000 Certified Facilities*. [Online]. Available: http://www.cepaa.org/certification.html [September 6, 2001].

[338] Chiquita Brands International, Inc. (May 2000). *Code of conduct . . . Living by our Core Values*. [Online]. Available: http://www.chiquita.com [June 23, 2001]. The Code of Conduct excepts from the child labor provisions "family farm suppliers in the company's seasonal, non-banana business." Ibid., p. 8.

[339] Ibid., p. 1.

quality and cost but also on their demonstrated achievement of these standards."[340]

In 2001, Chiquita also took the rare step of negotiating an agreement governing labor rights on Latin American banana plantations with international trade union bodies—the Latin American Coordination of Banana Worker Unions (COLSIBA), a regional coordination of banana worker unions with roughly 46,000 members, and the International Union of Food, Agricultural, Hotel, Restaurant, Catering, Tobacco and Allied Workers' Associations (IUF), an international trade union secretariat with approximately 2.5 million affiliated members.[341] Nonetheless, this agreement, signed at the ILO in Geneva and witnessed by Juan Somavia, director general of the organization, backtracks on Chiquita's commitment to ensure respect for labor rights on its third-party supplier plantations. The agreement states that Chiquita will require third-party suppliers "to provide reasonable evidence that they respect national legislation and the Minimum Labor Standards outlined in Part I of this agreement," but concedes that Chiquita's compliance with this provision will not be categorically demanded. Instead, the agreement provides, "[T]he effective implementation of this provision is dependent on a number of factors such as Chiquita's relative degree of influence over its suppliers and the availability of appropriate and commercially viable supply alternatives."[342] Ron Oswald, general secretary of IUF, told Human Rights Watch, however, that at least with respect to future purchasing contracts with suppliers, the IUF has "secured agreement in principle from Chiquita" that:

> Chiquita will include the terms of the agreement in the purchase contracts in such a way that they will have serious leverage on suppliers who do not respect the agreement. Such a contract can in an extreme case be relatively easily rescinded by Chiquita if it becomes clear that a particular supplier

---

[340] Chiquita Brands International, Inc., *2000 Corporate Responsibility Report* (September 2001), p. 72.

[341] Press Releases. (June 14, 2001). *IUF, COLSIBA and Chiquita Sign Historic Agreement on Trade Union Rights for Banana Workers.* [Online]. Available: http://www.chiquita.com/announcements [August 27, 2001]; Human Rights Watch telephone interview, Justo Pastor Reyes, training and workplace environment coordinator, COLSIBA, Honduras, September 25, 2001; Electronic communication from Ron Oswald, general secretary, IUF, to Human Rights Watch, September 2, 2001. The agreement was reached among Chiquita, COLSIBA, and IUF. "IUF/COLSIBA and Chiquita Agreement on Freedom of Association, Minimum Labour Standards and Employment in Latin American Banana Operations," June 14, 2001.

[342] "IUF/COLSIBA and Chiquita Agreement . . . ," June 14, 2001.

fails to respect the terms of the IUF/COLSIBA-Chiquita workers' rights agreement.[343]

If such a contract term had been included in contracts negotiated between Chiquita and the independent Ecuadorian suppliers from which it purchases occasionally, it could have helped to prevent the labor rights abuses described to Human Rights Watch by workers employed on those plantations.

Chiquita's sole primary suppliers in Ecuador are plantations of Favorita's banana-producing subsidiary, Reybancorp, all of which are "ECO-OK" certified.[344] Jeffrey Zalla, Chiquita's corporate responsibility officer, explained in a letter to Human Rights Watch, "Social and environmental responsibility issues were important in our selection of, and have helped to frame our ongoing relationship with, [Favorita] . . . as our principal banana supplier . . . in Ecuador," noting that Favorita "has chosen to follow Chiquita's own strict policies regarding the application of pesticides" and "provide[s] generous pay and benefits when compared to the rest of the industry in Ecuador."[345]

The ECO-OK seal is administered by the Conservation Agriculture Network (CAN), a coalition of independent conservation organizations in the Americas led by the U.S.-based Rainforest Alliance, that certifies individual banana plantations that are deemed to meet CAN's "Banana Standards and Indicators,"[346] which include the requirements that:

> Discrimination based on . . . sex . . . is not permitted; . . . Employees should be hired directly by the company. The hiring of temporary or seasonal employees through an intermediary for specific activities is only permitted in special cases, and these employees must be guaranteed the same rights and benefits as permanent employees; . . . Hiring minors is not permitted. The definition of minor is based on national law regarding agricultural activities, but may not be lower than 14; . . . Workers' right to

---

[343] Electronic communication from Ron Oswald to Human Rights Watch, October 16, 2001.

[344] Human Rights Watch interview, Ricardo Flores; Letter from Dr. Segundo Wong to Human Rights Watch, July 17, 2001.

[345] Letter from Jeffrey Zalla to Human Rights Watch, August 28, 2001; see also Chiquita Brands International, Inc., *2000 Corporate Responsibility Report*, . . . p. 73. In its *2000 Corporate Responsibility Report*, Chiquita also states that Favorita provides "social benefits including primary schooling, health and dental care for workers and their children up to age 15, and wage adjustments every six months to keep up with inflation."

[346] CAN, *Complete Standards for Banana Certification*, September 1999.

organize and negotiate freely with their superiors must be guaranteed; ... Work conditions must meet safety and health requirements.[347]

However, unlike SA8000 and Chiquita's code of conduct, the ECO-OK seal has no implications for a corporation's supply chain. Therefore, certification of all thirty-three of Reybancorp's banana plantations in Ecuador does not mean that Favorita's third-party suppliers, with whose administration Favorita has stated it "cannot interfere," are also ECO-OK-compliant. Furthermore, according to Jeffrey Zalla, although Chiquita stipulates in its contracts with Reybancorp "that the Chiquita fruit they provide must, as much as possible, be supplied from these certified farms," at times that is not possible.[348] Zalla notes, "In 2000 and year-to-date June 2001, 56% and 63%, respectively, of the fruit supplied to Chiquita from [Reybancorp] ... came from these certified farms."[349] Ricardo Flores, general manager of Chiquita's Ecuadorian subsidiary, explained that when fruit supplied to Chiquita does not come from certified Reybancorp plantations, Chiquita sends "people in the fields to check these plantations . . . the level of quality and agricultural practices . . . [but] nothing with regard to the rest. That part about workers and safety and health, we do not check."[350] Nonetheless, Zalla wrote to Human Rights Watch that "since 1999 Chiquita has . . . conducted its own periodic sample assessments of the social and environmental performance of the [Favorita] . . . farms *and those of its suppliers* in Ecuador" [emphasis added].[351] Thirty-three children with whom Human Rights Watch spoke reported working on such supplier plantations. According to information provided to Human Rights Watch by Zalla, however, Chiquita was supplied by plantations that Human Rights Watch determined employed only four of those thirty-three children.[352]

---

[347] Ibid., paras. 3.1.1, 3.1.2, 3.1.4, 3.2.1, 3.3.2.

[348] Letter from Jeffrey Zalla to Human Rights Watch, August 28, 2001.

[349] Ibid. Zalla explained, however, "Even more fruit would come from these farms were it not for the fact that our ships must typically be loaded within 2 days while a normal farm harvest occurs over 5 days."

[350] Human Rights Watch interview, Ricardo Flores.

[351] Letter from Jeffrey Zalla to Human Rights Watch, August 28, 2001.

[352] Ibid.

Favorita

As discussed above, Reybancorp's thirty-three directly owned plantations are ECO-OK certified. According to an ECO-OK manual produced by the Conservation and Development Corporation, a member of CAN administering the ECO-OK program in Ecuador, all the above-listed ECO-OK conditions must be fulfilled by Ecuadorian certified plantations.[353] In practice, however, Reybancorp's plantations are ECO-OK certified despite their admitted use of subcontractors to employ approximately 87 percent of their workforce. Far from "special cases," subcontracted workers are used, according to Favorita's executive vice president, as part of everyday operations at Reybancorp, to obtain "flexibility" and for "reasonable administrative management."[354] Nevertheless, these ECO-OK standards do not govern the independent plantations supplying Favorita on which workers interviewed by Human Rights Watch allegedly labored, as ECO-OK certification has no implications for Favorita's third-party supplier plantations.

Favorita and the International Finance Corporation

On May 29, 1998, the International Finance Corporation approved investment of U.S. $15 million to "expand production capacities . . . and enhance international competitiveness of Reybanpac."[355] Project summary information indicates that environmental and occupational safety and health conditions on plantations of Reybancorp, Favorita's banana-producing subsidiary, were reviewed prior to project approval, including pesticide use, handling of hazardous materials, and "general worker health and safety."[356] This project was formally appraised by the IFC according to its policies in place at the time, which did not include the "Policy Statement on Harmful Child and

---

[353] Ríos F., Ed., Programa de Certificación ECO-OK, *Manual de Operación para Manejo Integral de Plantaciones de Banano* [ECO-OK Certification Program, *Manual of Operation for Integrated Management of Banana Plantations*] (Quito: Corporación de Conservación y Desarrollo (CCD), 1999), pp. 20-22.

[354] Human Rights Watch interview, Vicente Wong. When asked about the subcontracting restrictions in the ECO-OK certification criteria, a representative of CCD told Human Rights Watch that the criteria did not apply in Ecuador because Ecuadorian law permits the use of subcontractors. Human Rights Watch interview, José Valdivieso, CCD, Quito, May 8, 2001.

[355] IFC. (No date). *Summary of Project Information*. [Online]. Available: http://wbln0018.worldbank.org/IFCExt/spiwebsite1.nsf [September 11, 2001].

[356] Ibid.

Forced Labor" adopted in March 1998.[357] Since the policy is not retroactive, the project is not governed by the modest terms of the child labor policy nor its "Interim Guidance," which recognizes that "problems of harmful child labor may exist with suppliers" and encourages, but does not require, IFC clients to review major supplier relationships and ask suppliers to "address" instances of harmful child labor.[358] Nonetheless, according to an IFC official, "our appraisal

---

[357] Ibid.; Electronic communication from Dr. Kerry Connor, senior social specialist, IFC Environmental and Social Development Department, to Human Rights Watch, October 23, 2001.

[358] IFC. (March 1998). *Harmful Child Labor: Interim Guidance*. [Online]. Before obtaining approval, the project, nonetheless, was required to fulfill the terms of the IFC's "Exclusion List," which prohibits IFC funding for "[p]roduction or activities involving harmful or exploitative forms of forced labor/harmful child labor." But this provision is narrowly interpreted as applicable to the final goods or services rendered, rather than the conditions under which they were produced or provided. For example, a project involving the production of child pornography would be prohibited because the final product is harmful to children. However, funding for a textile factory using exploitative child labor would be acceptable since the final product is clothing. The Favorita project, therefore, satisfied the list's child labor provision, as bananas were its final product. Since adoption of the IFC's child labor policy, projects continue to undergo early review according to "Exclusion List" requirements and are later appraised according to child labor policy criteria. IFC. (December 1998). *Environmental & Social Review Procedure Annex A: Exclusion List*. [Online]. Available: http://www.ifc.org/enviro/enviro/

and supervision indicate that [the Favorita project] complies with the IFC's social and environmental policies, including the current policy on harmful child labor."[359] However, fourteen of the children with whom Human Rights Watch spoke had worked on plantations that one or more workers alleged occasionally supplied Favorita. Although Human Rights Watch sent a letter to Favorita inquiring whether the company had purchased fruit from the two plantations on which these children labored, Favorita responded without confirming or denying the contractual relationships.[360]

Review_Procedure_Main/Review_Procedure/Annex_A/ annex_a.htm [October 3, 2001]; IFC. (December 1998). *Environmental & Social Review Procedure.* [Online]. Available: http://www.ifc.org/enviro/EnvSoc/ESRP/esrp.htm [October 22, 2001].

[359] Electronic communication from Dr. Kerry Connor to Human Rights Watch.

[360] Letter from Dr. Segundo Wong to Human Rights Watch, July 17, 2001.

VII. BANANA EXPORTS AND TRADE REGIMES

Human Rights Watch believes that there is an inherent link between labor rights and trade. When countries or regions engage in trade, they have a fundamental obligation to ensure that the goods being traded are not produced in violation of internationally recognized labor rights, including freedom of association and the prohibition of the worst forms of child labor. As the two largest importers of Ecuadorian bananas, importing in 2000 roughly one million metric tons and 680,000 metric tons of Ecuadorian bananas, respectively,[361] the United States and the European Union should be able to guarantee that trade provisions governing the import of Ecuadorian bananas include provisions that ensure respect for the labor rights of banana workers in Ecuador. Nevertheless, because of the current structure of U.S. and E.U. tariff arrangements for the importation of Ecuadorian bananas, such conditionality is likely precluded by the terms of the World Trade Organization (WTO), of which the United States, E.U. countries, and Ecuador are members.

In the United States, Ecuadorian bananas enter unconditionally duty free under column one of the Harmonized Tariff Schedule (HTS), published by the United States International Trade Commission. The HTS provides the applicable tariff rates for all goods entering the United States, and, in particular, in column one establishes the general tariff rate for countries that have normal trade relations (NTR) with the United States.[362] Ecuadorian goods covered by the United States Generalized System of Preferences (U.S. GSP) or the Andean Trade Preferences Act (ATPA), to which Ecuador is party, may enter the United States duty free only if the exporting country has taken or is taking "steps to afford internationally recognized worker rights . . . to workers in the country."[363]

---

[361] Human Rights Watch telephone interview, Robert Miller, USDA. In 2000, these totals constituted approximately 24 percent and 17 percent of Ecuador's banana exports, respectively.

[362] United States International Trade Commission (USITC), "Harmonized Tariff Schedule of the United States (2001)," *USITC Publication 3378* (2001), chapter 8-3; USITC, "Andean Trade Preferences Act: Impact on the United States," *USITC Publication 3234* (September 1999), pp. 69, 75. NTR is the norm in the United States' bilateral trade relationships, and the U.S. has extended NTR status to all WTO members as well as most other nations. International Trade Data System. (August 17, 2001). *Normal Trade Relations.* [Online]. Available: http://www.itds.tread.gov/mfn.htm [September 10, 2001].

[363] 19 U.S.C. § 2462(b)(2)(G); 19 U.S.C. § 3202(c)(7). "Internationally recognized worker rights," in this context, are defined to include the right of association; the right to organize and bargain collectively; a prohibition on the use of any form of forced or compulsory labor; a minimum age for the employment of children; and acceptable conditions of work with respect to minimum wages, hours of work, and occupational safety and health. 19 U.S.C. § 2467(4). In addition, goods covered by U.S. GSP may

But there is no such requirement for goods, like bananas, entering the United States unconditionally duty free under the Harmonized Tariff Schedule.

From 1993 through June 2001, the European Union's importation scheme for bananas was characterized by complicated tariff-rate quotas—tariffs that vary according to the volume of bananas imported—as well as complex licensing schemes, and, at times, various country-specific quotas. These provisions were successfully challenged before the WTO. In July 2001, after several WTO rulings that the European Union's system did not comply with WTO norms, the European Union began a process to transfer to a pure tariff system for the importation of bananas by 2006. Ecuador's tariff access to the E.U. market for bananas, like the U.S. market, is not influenced by Ecuador's protection of internationally recognized labor rights, as fresh bananas are not covered by the European Union's GSP legislation;[364] the European Union has not negotiated an independent trade agreement with Ecuador; and Ecuador does not qualify for the European Union's tariff benefits for "least developed countries."[365]

As stated, Human Rights Watch believes that linking tariff benefits and workers' rights is critical to the promotion of internationally recognized labor rights. However, governments' WTO obligations may prevent such linkage. Under the WTO, a member country may provide more favorable treatment to another's products under regional free-trade agreements, like the ATPA, or under special trade regimes for developing countries, like GSP.[366] But, under articles I and XII of the General Agreement on Tariffs and Trade (GATT), a country must treat a product from one WTO member country neither more nor less favorably than that same product from another WTO member country in most other cases.[367] Since U.S. and E.U. tariff rates governing the importation

---

enter the United States duty free only if the exporting country has also "implemented its commitments to eliminate the worst forms of child labor." 19 U.S.C. § 2462(b)(2)(H).

[364] As in the United States, fresh bananas are not covered by the European Union's GSP regime, though plantains, fresh and dried, and dried bananas are covered. Under this regime, GSP benefits may be withdrawn in cases of slavery, forced labor, "serious and systematic violation of the [right of] freedom of association, the right to collective bargaining or the principle of non-discrimination in respect of employment and occupation, or use of child labour, as defied in the relevant ILO Conventions," or if exported products were made with prison labor. Council Regulation (EC) No. 2501/2001, December 10, 2001, Articles 4, 26; Annex IV.

[365] Council Regulation (EEC) No 416/2001, February 28, 2001, Annex IV.

[366] WTO. (No date). *Relevant WTO provisions: descriptions*. [Online]. Available: http:///www.wto.org [September 10, 2001].

[367] General Agreement on Tariffs and Trade, July 1986, Articles I:1, XIII: 1.

of Ecuadorian bananas are established neither by trade agreements nor by trade regimes for developing countries, the United States and the European Union are likely precluded from revoking duty-free treatment or providing less favorable treatment for Ecuadorian bananas based on labor rights abuses in that country's banana sector. Unless article XX of the GATT, the WTO provision allowing a country to restrict importation of a product to protect public morals or human health, is interpreted to permit import restriction based on the export country's failure to protect internationally recognized workers' rights, the United States and the European Union have little leverage with which to demand that Ecuadorian bananas eaten by their consumers are not produced by workers whose labor rights are violated.[368]

European Union Banana Importation Regimes

In 1993, the European Union introduced the Common Market Organization for Bananas, attempting to unify an assortment of bilateral trade agreements among individual E.U. member states and their African, Caribbean, and Pacific (ACP) former colonies.[369] The agreements provided preferential quotas for all supplier ACP countries and, in addition, special licensing treatment and individual country quotas for the twelve traditional ACP banana suppliers— Belize, Cameroon, Cape Verde, Ivory Coast, Dominica, Grenada, Jamaica, Somalia, St. Lucia, St. Vincent, the Grenadines, and Suriname.[370] All ACP countries enjoyed duty-free treatment up to their quota limits.[371] Non-ACP countries, including Ecuador, enjoyed the less beneficial "Most Favored Nation" (MFN) tariff.[372] This preferential treatment protected ACP banana producers, typically small family farms with difficult terrain, which would have had

---

[368] Ibid., Article XX (a), (b).

[369] Council Regulation (EEC), No. 404/93, February 13, 1993.

[370] Raj Bhala, "The Bananas War," 31 *McGeorge Law Review* 3 (2000), in Raj Bhala, *International Trade Law: Theory and Practice* (Danvers, Massachusetts: Matthew Bender & Company, Inc., 2000), p. 1466. The system distinguishes among the traditional ACP countries, listed above; non-traditional ACP countries, such as the Dominican Republic, Ghana, and Kenya; and non-ACP countries, which encompass all other countries, including those in Latin America.

[371] Ibid., pp. 1465, 1469-70.

[372] Roland Herrmann, Marc Kramb, Christina Monnich. (December 2000). *Tariff Rate Quotas and the Economic Impacts of Agricultural Trade Liberalization in the WTO*. [Online]. Available: http://www.uni-giessen.de/zeu/DiscPap1.pdf [July 31, 2001], p. 15.

difficulty competing with flat and fertile Latin American plantations with highly integrated marketing and production.[373]

Latin American banana-exporting countries objected to this special treatment, however. Colombia, Costa Rica, Nicaragua, and Venezuela negotiated a Framework Agreement on Bananas (BFA) with the European Union, which entered into force in 1995 and provided each nation with a country-specific import quota.[374] In exchange, the four countries agreed not to bring a case against the European Union before the WTO until 2002.[375] Nevertheless, Ecuador, Guatemala, Honduras, Mexico, and the United States, not part of the BFA, filed a complaint before the WTO in 1996, alleging that the E.U. regime for importing bananas violated the GATT. A panel report issued by the WTO on September 9, 1997 agreed and ordered the import regime amended.[376] In October 1997, the WTO's appellate body affirmed the panel's conclusions.[377]

In an attempt to comply with the WTO ruling, the European Union revised its banana importation regime in January 1999.[378] The new system continued to rely on tariff-rate quotas and complex licensing schemes but allocated over 90 percent of non-APC country quotas to the "substantial suppliers" of E.U. bananas, with Ecuador receiving 26.2 percent, Costa Rica 25.6 percent,

---

[373] See, e.g., House of Commons. (January 14, 1998). *Select Committee on European Legislation: Sixteenth Report*. [Online]. Available: http://www.parliament.the-stationery-off [July 31, 2001].

[374] Costa Rica received 23.4 percent, Colombia 21.0 percent, Nicaragua 3.0 percent, and Venezuela 2.0 percent of the quota for third-country banana suppliers. Herrmann, Kramb, Monnich. (December 2000). *Tariff Rate Quotas and the Economic Impacts of Agricultural Trade Liberalization in the WTO*. [Online]. . . . , p. 17.

[375] Bhala, "The Bananas War ," . . . , pp. 1464, 1469.

[376] European Communities—Regime for the Importation, Sale and Distribution of Bananas: Ecuador's Complaint: Report of the Panel, WTO Doc. WT/DS27/R/ECU, May 22, 1997.

[377] European Communities—Regime for the Importation, Sale and Distribution of Bananas: Report of the Appellate Body, WTO Doc. WT/DS27/AB/R, September 9, 1997, pp. 162-63. The WTO found that among the violated provisions were GATT Article XIII:1, which states that a country may not restrict the importation of a product from one member without similarly restricting importation of that product from all other members, and the Most Favored Nation clause, Article I:1, which requires that any "advantage, favour, privilege or immunity" granted to one country with respect to a certain product be granted to all member countries with respect to that product. Ibid.; GATT, Articles XIII:1, I:1.

[378] "US Government and European Commission Reach Agreement to Resolve Long-Standing Banana Dispute," *European Union News Release*, April 11, 2001.

Colombia 23.0 percent, and Panama 15.8 percent.[379] This new scheme, however, was also found to violate the WTO, and in April 1999, the WTO authorized the United States to impose trade sanctions of U.S. $191 million against the European Union, which the United States did.[380] In March 2000, Ecuador also sought and obtained authorization to impose sanctions but abstained from using them.[381]

After protracted negotiations, on April 11, 2001, the United States and the European Union agreed on a new E.U. banana importation regime, and the United States agreed to suspend sanctions and work to secure WTO authorization for the agreement.[382] Through a two-stage process involving shifting tariff-rate quotas and licensing allocations based on companies' histories of supplying the European Union and their import/export practices,[383] the new importation scheme is designed to phase in a tariff-only system by 2006.[384] Until 2006, however, traditional ACP countries will continue to have their own tariff-rate quota and licensing preferences, but all individual country quotas are abolished.[385] After initially objecting to this plan, Ecuador reached an agreement with the European Union, which, though not altering the structure of the new trade regime, addressed Ecuador's primary concerns by designing a system for allocating import licenses to protect Ecuadorian small and medium producers' license access.[386] In return, Ecuador forfeited its right to impose

---

[379] Herrmann, Kramb, Monnich. (December 2000). *Tariff Rate Quotas and the Economic Impacts of Agricultural Trade Liberalization in the WTO.* [Online]. . . . , p. 17; World Bank, Project SICA, Agricultural Information, System Ministry of Agriculture and Livestock—Ecuador. (No date). *Regime on Principal Markets: The Banana Regime of the European Union in Force as of January 1, 1999.* [Online]. Available: http://www.sica.gov.ec/ingles/cadenas/banano/docs/reglam1637.htm [August 1, 2001].

[380] "US Government and European Commission Reach Agreement . . . ," *European Union News Release.*

[381] Eliza Patterson, "The US-E.U. Agreement to Resolve the Banana Dispute," *ASIL Insight: US-E.U. Banana Dispute Agreement*, April 2001.

[382] "US Government and European Commission Reach Agreement . . . ," *European Union News Release.* The United States lifted sanctions on July 1, 2001. "USTR Removes Duties on E.U. Goods Imposed in Banana Dispute," *Market News International*, July 2, 2001.

[383] "Understanding on Bananas," *European Union Press Release*, April 30, 2001.

[384] Patterson, "The US-E.U. Agreement . . . ," *ASIL Insight: US-E.U. Banana Dispute Agreement.*

[385] "Understanding on Bananas," *European Union Press Release.*

[386] Ibid.; "Commission Approves Banana Regs. After Settling with Ecuador," *Inside U.S. Trade*, May 4, 2001, p. 19. Dole, Ecuador's second largest exporter, had also objected to

sanctions on the European Union and abandoned its efforts to prevent the European Union from obtaining a WTO waiver to allow temporary preferential treatment of ACP countries.[387] Under the tariff-only system, scheduled to begin in 2006, Ecuador will compete freely against other banana-producing countries for access to the E.U. market, as it does now for U.S. market access.

---

the licensing scheme because license allocation, until December 2003, is to be based on E.U. market share between 1994 and 1996, a period during which Dole's importation of Ecuadorian bananas in the European Union was significantly lower than in later years.

[387] "Understanding on Bananas," *European Union Press Release*.

VIII. SPECIFIC RECOMMENDATIONS

Human Rights Watch makes the following specific recommendations to suggest concrete steps to remedy Ecuador's violations of its international legal obligations and to address the conduct of banana-exporting corporations and their local banana suppliers that allows them to benefit from these violations.

To the Government of Ecuador: Preventing the Worst Forms of Child Labor

Legal and labor reforms
Finding: Despite the Worst Forms of Child Labour Convention requirement that countries define, in consultation with employers' and workers' organizations, and prohibit work "likely to harm the health, safety or morals of children," the Labor Code fails to prohibit explicitly the performance of certain tasks and work under conditions hazardous to children. Only if very broadly construed could the effective enforcement of existing Ecuadorian law governing child labor prevent children from working in all conditions and performing all tasks that constitute the worst forms of child labor.

Recommendation: Although the Labor Code prohibits children from work that can be harmful to "physical, mental, spiritual, moral, or social development" and bans children from "handling psychotropic or toxic objects or substances" or performing tasks considered "dangerous or unhealthy," Congress should amend the law, as an interim step to achieving full compliance with the Worst Forms of Child Labour Convention, to explicitly prohibit all individuals under the age of eighteen from using dangerous tools, from handling pesticides and pesticide-treated products, and from being exposed to pesticides in the workplace through third-party application or aerial fumigation.

Recommendation: The Ministry of Labor in coordination with the Ministry of Agriculture should ensure that restricted-entry intervals (REIs)—the time after pesticide application when entry into the treated area is banned or limited—are clearly established in government regulations and vigorously enforced and, as a preliminary step to achieving compliance with the Worst Forms of Child Labour Convention, include special REIs for children, taking into consideration the greater risks they face from exposure to toxic chemicals.

Recommendation: Following the suggestion of the Worst Forms of Child Labour Recommendation that special attention be given to girls and recognizing that sexual harassment is a form of sex discrimination, Congress should amend the

Ecuadorian Labor Code to prohibit sexual harassment in the workplace. It should define sexual harassment in accordance with the definition adopted by the United Nation's Committee on the Elimination of All Forms of Discrimination against Women and establish separate and more stringent penalties for cases in which the victim of sexual harassment is a minor.

Enforcement
Finding: The Ministry of Labor fails to enforce effectively laws governing the human rights of child workers, including the minimum age and maximum hours for child workers, limits on tasks children may perform, school completion requirements, health and safety conditions for children in the workplace, and access at work to potable water and sanitation facilities.

Recommendation: The Labor Inspectorate of the Ministry of Labor should fulfill its responsibility to enforce all Labor Code provisions governing and relevant to child labor. As a first step to achieving effective enforcement, Ecuador should uphold its obligations under article 10 of the ILO Labour Inspection Convention, which states, "The number of labour inspectors shall be sufficient to secure the effective discharge of the duties of the inspectorate." As a state party to the convention, Ecuador should allocate additional resources to the Labor Inspectorate to provide for a sufficient number of inspectors to guarantee effective implementation of child labor laws through proactive monitoring and unannounced on-site inspections rather than reliance on a complaint-driven enforcement strategy.

Recommendation: As a preliminary step towards fulfilling Ecuador's ILO Labour Inspection Convention obligations, the Ministry of Labor should, as required by Ecuadorian law, designate one or more labor inspectors for minors in each province. In accordance with article 7(3) of the convention, which provides that "[l]abour inspectors shall be adequately trained for the performance of their duties," the government should ensure that these inspectors receive sufficient funding and other resources and specialized training to enforce child labor laws.

Recommendation: The Labor Inspectorate should ensure that, as an interim step to achieving full compliance with the Worst Forms of Child Labour Convention, all workers, including children, receive full information and training from their employers about occupational illnesses and injuries related to work on banana plantations, including those associated with exposure to pesticides. The Labor Inspectorate should guarantee that trainings are conducted regularly and in a manner understandable to children, in compliance with Ecuadorian law that requires that employers not only provide workers with appropriate protective equipment but train them on the correct means of protecting themselves from workplace hazards and ensure that "labor conditions . . . do not present a danger to [workers'] health or life."

Recommendation: As required by the Worst Forms of Child Labour Convention, Ecuador should "design and implement programmes of action to eliminate as a priority the worst forms of child labour . . . in consultation with relevant government institutions and employers' and workers' organizations." In particular, the National Council for Children and Adolescents, the National Directorate for Protection of Minors, juvenile courts, and the Ministry of Labor, along with the National Committee for the Progressive Elimination of Child Labor, in coordination with community-based workers' and employers' organizations, should take concrete steps to give effect to the general regulation for implementation of the Minors' Code that recommends the establishment of programs "for protection, defense, and promotion of the rights of child workers . . . in the rural sector." Such programs could include labor rights education for children and their parents in rural areas, development of legislative reform proposals that address the problem of child labor in the rural sector, and coordination with the International Programme on the Elimination of Child Labour (IPEC) to develop programs for rural child workers.

Finding: The Ministry of Labor fails to keep data on the number of child laborers in Ecuador's banana sector. Although the National Institute of Statistics and Census (INEC) signed an agreement with the ILO's Statistical Information and Monitoring Programme on Child Labour (SIMPOC) in June 2001 to implement a national child labor survey, which began in August 2001, this survey will not disaggregate data by occupation. Without reliable statistics defining the scope and scale of child labor in the banana sector, it will be difficult for the government or other institutions to design programs and allocate sufficient resources to address the problem.

Recommendation: In accordance with the proposal in the ILO Recommendation concerning the Prohibition and Immediate Elimination of the Worst Forms of Child Labour that countries keep "detailed information and statistical data on the nature and extent of child labour" and "[a]s far as possible, . . . include data disaggregated by sex [and] occupation," the Ministry of Labor, in cooperation with INEC and SIMPOC, should undertake a comprehensive survey to determine the scope and scale of child labor in the banana sector, disaggregate the data by sex, and update the data regularly.

Finding: Pesticides potentially harmful to children are used on banana plantations that supply exporting corporations, and, in some cases, those corporations have approved application of those pesticides. Human Rights Watch believes that when child workers laboring on these plantations experience serious adverse health effects from pesticide exposure, the corporations and local suppliers are complicit in the violation of those children's right to health. When the illnesses suffered are caused by corporate-sanctioned pesticides, Human Rights Watch considers the corporations' complicity in the violation of children's rights is heightened.

Recommendation: As a preliminary measure to ensure that child workers are not exposed to hazardous substances, independent local plantation owners and banana-exporting corporations, in coordination with the Ministry of Agriculture, should conduct a joint survey of the health impact on children of exposure to the pesticides used on banana plantations, with a particular focus on corporate-sanctioned pesticides.

Recommendation: As an interim step to achieving full compliance with the Worst Forms of Child Labour Convention, the Ministry of Labor should guarantee that child banana workers whose health is damaged by pesticide exposure have access to free health care. To these ends, the Ministry of Labor should actively enforce Labor Code articles 359 and 371 that require employers to ensure free medical treatment for their workers, not covered by social security, who suffer workplaces accidents and illnesses.

To the Government of Ecuador: Protecting the Right to Freedom of Association

Finding: The ILO's Committee of Experts on the Application of Conventions and Recommendations has stated that the best solution for anti-union dismissal is generally the reinstatement of the affected worker with payment of lost wages; where reinstatement is impossible, compensation for anti-union dismissal should be higher than that prescribed for other kinds of dismissal. In Ecuador, an employer who fires a worker for engaging in union activity is not required to reinstate the wronged worker and, in most cases, is only subject to a small fine if the labor law violation is confirmed and a sanction imposed. The fine is usually no greater than the amount owed by an employer for dismissing a worker for any cause not recognized by the Labor Code as an acceptable reason for dismissal.

Recommendation: Congress should amend the Labor Code to require the reinstatement of permanent workers fired for engaging in union activity and payment of wages lost during the period when the workers were wrongfully dismissed. Where reinstatement is impossible, compensation for dismissal should be substantially higher than for other illegal terminations.

Recommendation: Congress should amend the Labor Code to provide explicitly that temporary workers or workers with project contracts who are fired for exercising the right to freedom of association have the right to reinstatement until the conclusion of their short-term contracts and to payment of any lost wages incurred during the period of wrongful dismissal. Where reinstatement is impossible, workers should receive meaningful compensation for the anti-union dismissal.

Finding: Inadequate government enforcement of the Labor Code combined with its ambiguity thwarts the law's intent to cap temporary employment contracts, negotiated to satisfy an "increase in demand for production or services," at 180 consecutive days. Weak Labor Code enforcement also frustrates the law's requirement that all project contracts for the performance of regular workplace activities last, at a minimum, for one year. Employers, both companies and subcontractors, often hire workers informally to labor on the same plantations or in the same work teams for many months or years on end, using consecutive temporary contracts or project contracts to create a precarious and vulnerable "permanent temporary" workforce. These workers enjoy no job stability and lack effective protection against anti-union discrimination.

Recommendation: The requirement that a temporary contract only be negotiated to satisfy exigent circumstances, such as the temporary absence of personnel, or to meet an "increase in demand for production or services" should be strictly enforced by the Labor Inspectorate, and the burden of proof should be placed on the employer to demonstrate, in each case, the existence of such circumstances. "An increase in demand for production or services" should be narrowly construed and defined to require a meaningful increase. In particular, an employer should be explicitly prohibited from asserting the existence of such an increase for more than 180 consecutive days.

Recommendation: To make the letter of the law conform with its spirit, Congress should amend the Labor Code to prohibit not only the use of temporary contracts with durations of over 180 consecutive days but also the use of consecutive, short-term temporary contracts adding up to more than 180 consecutive days to satisfy employers' demand increases. To these ends, as these short-term contracts are often executed for less than full five-day work weeks and may not require performance of the same tasks each day or each week, contracts for "180 consecutive days" should be understood as employment for the performance of any task, for any number of days per week, for roughly half a year—twenty-six consecutive weeks.

Recommendation: The requirement that all project contracts for the performance of regular workplace activities, such as the everyday tasks of banana workers in packing plants and banana fields, last, at a minimum, for one year should be vigorously enforced by the Labor Inspectorate.

Recommendation: In the few cases in which collective bargaining agreements have been negotiated on banana plantations, the Labor Inspectorate should ensure that the terms and conditions of the agreements are applicable to all workers, temporary and permanent, regardless of whether they are affiliated with the workers' organizations party to the agreements, as required by Labor Code article 224 and a Supreme Court of Justice resolution that establish that a collective agreement protects all workers in a workplace.

Finding: The Constitution provides that when workers are hired by a subcontractor, the "person for whose benefit work is realized" is jointly responsible for compliance with labor law obligations. Nevertheless, workers employed by a subcontractor are not permitted to organize and collectively bargain with the "person for whose benefit work is realized," who often controls the workers' salaries, benefits, and health and safety conditions. Instead, the subcontracted workers can only legally organize and negotiate collectively with their subcontractors. As recognized by the ILO Convention concerning the Right to Organise and Collective Bargaining, however, collective bargaining should occur "with a view to the regulation of terms and conditions of employment."

Recommendation: Congress should amend the Labor Code to allow subcontracted workers to organize and bargain collectively with the person or company for whose benefit work is realized if that person or company, in practice, has the economic power to dictate, directly or indirectly, the workers' terms and conditions of employment.

Finding: In 1991, the Ecuadorian Labor Code was amended to raise the minimum number of workers required for the formation of a workers' organization from fifteen to thirty. This high thirty-worker mandatory minimum enables employers to attain significant business growth—up to twenty-nine employees—and preserve a union-free workplace. The ILO has twice recommended that Ecuador reduce the number, noting that Ecuador "has a very large proportion of small enterprises."

Recommendation: The Ministry of Labor should undertake a survey to determine the number of employers with fewer than thirty workers in the banana sector and update the data regularly.

Recommendation: Congress should amend the Labor Code to reduce the minimum number of workers required to form a union, pursuant to the ILO's recommendations.

To Banana-Exporting Corporations and Local Suppliers

Finding: Corporations export over four million metric tons of Ecuadorian bananas annually, a significant percentage of which are supplied by third-party plantations. When labor rights abuses occur on these plantations and exporting corporations fail to take remedial steps to ensure respect for workers' rights, these companies facilitate and benefit from the violations. Therefore, exporting corporations, in addition to independent local plantation owners, have an obligation to ensure that workers' rights are upheld on companies' independent supplier plantations.

Recommendation: Exporting corporations, in coordination with their independent local suppliers, should ensure that pesticides potentially harmful to children are neither sanctioned for use nor applied in practice on supplier plantations.

Recommendation: In the event that corporations discover violations of Ecuadorian labor law or international labor standards on supplier plantations, the corporations should immediately turn this information over to the appropriate Ecuadorian authorities.

Recommendation: When exporting corporations find children under fifteen working on their directly owned or third-party supplier plantations, they, in coordination with the independent local suppliers, should provide adequate support for those children to attend school or a suitable academic alternative until they reach age fifteen, in accordance with the Constitution that mandates schooling for children under fifteen. When those children are under fourteen, the minimum age of employment established by the Labor Code, adequate support should be provided for them to attend school or an appropriate academic alternative in lieu of working.

Recommendation: Dole, a signatory member of the workplace code of conduct SA8000, should fulfill its public commitment to monitor labor conditions, including freedom of association and child labor, on third-party supplier plantations; begin to bring all suppliers, both long-term and sporadic, into compliance with Ecuadorian labor law and SA8000 standards as soon as possible and at least within the reasonable period of 180 days; and report publicly on such efforts on at least an annual basis.

Recommendation: Chiquita, which has incorporated into its company code of conduct most of SA8000's terms, should fulfill its public commitment to monitor labor conditions, including freedom of association and child labor, on its third-party supplier plantations; begin to bring all suppliers, both long-term and sporadic, into compliance with Ecuadorian labor law and its company code of conduct as soon as possible and at least within the reasonable period of 180 days; and report publicly on such efforts on at least an annual basis.

Recommendation: Chiquita should ensure that all external agreements negotiated with trade union bodies or other third parties that address labor rights on Chiquita's supplier plantations, like the "IUF/COLSIBA and Chiquita Agreement on Freedom of Association, Minimum Labour Standards and Employment in Latin American Banana Operations," meet or exceed the standards set forth in the company's internal code of conduct.

To the International Labor Organization and the United Nations Children's Fund

Finding: Ecuador has signed a Memorandum of Understanding with the ILO's International Programme on the Elimination of Child Labour, a program that works progressively to eliminate child labor, largely by strengthening national capacities to address child labor issues. IPEC has developed action programs in

Ecuador to address the issues of street children, children in brick-making, and children laboring in small-scale traditional mining, and Quito's Construction Chamber (Cámara de Construcción de Quito) has signed an agreement with IPEC to finance economic feasibility studies for the brick-making sector programs.

Recommendation: IPEC should consider expanding its work in Ecuador to include action programs and other initiatives to address child labor in the banana sector and should negotiate agreements with banana-exporting corporations in which the corporations commit to providing financial assistance to these activities.

Finding: In 2001, the United States Congress appropriated U.S. $45 million to IPEC to focus on five objectives, one of which is "[e]liminating child labor in specific hazardous and/or abusive occupations" with an aim to "remove children from work, provide them with educational opportunities, and generate alternative sources of income for their families." No such program has been developed to address child labor on Ecuador's banana plantations.

Recommendation: IPEC should develop and implement such a project in Ecuador's banana sector in cooperation with the government, labor and banana industry groups, and nongovernmental organizations.

Finding: Although SIMPOC's national child labor survey, begun in August 2001, will document the number of children working in the agriculture sector, the data will not indicate how many of those rural child laborers are banana workers.

Recommendation: Through its national child labor survey, SIMPOC should gather statistics that demonstrate the scope and scale of child labor in the banana industry and should use Rapid Assessment Methodology—an alternative to scientifically designed statistical methods of data collection designed to obtain information quickly on child labor in a particular setting—to develop a quantitative and qualitative profile of child labor in the banana sector.

Finding: As part of its "Medium-term strategic plan, 2002-2005" (MTSP), UNICEF has identified improved protection of children from violence, exploitation, abuse, and discrimination as one of five priorities. Within the area of exploitation, eliminating the worst forms of child labor is a particular focus.

Recommendation: In accordance with the MTSP, the UNICEF country office in Ecuador should establish effective national, local, and community-based systems to monitor child labor in the banana sector, develop, support, and realize program interventions to end child labor practices in that sector contrary to international standards, and implement recovery and reintegration programs for affected children.

To Countries Engaged in or Preparing to Engage in Trade with Ecuador

Finding: Ecuador is the largest banana exporter in the world. When its bananas enter the global marketplace, many have been produced in violation of internationally recognized labor rights, including freedom of association and the prohibition of the worst forms of child labor.

Recommendation: International trade agreements to which Ecuador is a party and trade regimes governing the importation of Ecuadorian bananas should include provisions that ensure respect for internationally recognized workers' rights, including the right to freedom of association and the prohibition of the worst forms of child labor. In trade agreements, failure to effectively enforce or progressively implement such standards should trigger the same dispute settlement, enforcement procedures, or penalties available to other issues covered by these agreements.

To International Financial Institutions

Finding: The International Finance Corporation's (IFC's), a member of the World Bank Group, in March 1998, adopted its "Policy Statement on Harmful Child and Forced Labor," with "Interim Guidance" that encourages companies receiving IFC financing to review major supplier relationships and ask suppliers to "address" instances of harmful child labor.

Recommendation: Although the IFC "Policy Statement on Harmful Child and Forced Labor" also states, "Projects should comply with the national laws of the host countries, including those that protect core labor standards and related treaties ratified by the host countries," the IFC should expand the policy to provide explicitly that the IFC will not support projects in which the ILO Declaration on Fundamental Principles and Rights at Work is violated.

Recommendation: The IFC should revise its "Policy Statement on Harmful Child and Forced Labor" to make investment assistance contingent on beneficiary corporations' respect for the internationally recognized workers' rights set forth in the ILO Declaration on Fundamental Principles and Rights at Work, which include the right to "freedom of association" and the "effective abolition of child labour"—both in enterprises directly owned by the corporations and in third-party supplier enterprises.

Recommendation: The IFC should ensure that any IFC projects that invest in corporations exporting bananas from Ecuador conduct reviews of labor practices both on the corporations' directly owned plantations as well as independent supplier plantations during initial project appraisals and ongoing supervision and make investment conditional on respect for internationally recognized labor rights on those plantations.

Finding: In the past decade, the Inter-American Development Bank (IADB) and the World Bank have funded a number of programs in Ecuador's rural and agricultural sectors. In the project appraisal for its program approved July 2001, "Rural Poverty Alleviation and Local Development Project," the World Bank noted, "Public regulatory and administrative institutions are weak and inefficient" and "the economic crisis has severely reduced government resources." Nevertheless, none of the IADB or World Bank programs have dedicated resources to address the failure of Ecuador's Ministry of Labor to enforce domestic labor laws in the banana sector.

Recommendation: In consultation with the ILO, the World Bank and/or IADB should fund a project in Ecuador that provides technical support and capacity building assistance for the Ministry of Labor to enforce labor legislation effectively in the banana sector.

IX. CONCLUSION

Human Rights Watch takes no position on trade nor globalization per se, but instead believes that the two must not occur at the expense of the labor rights of workers producing goods for the global stream of commerce. National governments, exporting corporations, and importing countries have a responsibility to demand respect for the internationally recognized labor rights of these workers from whose toil they all reap rewards. The Ecuadorian government and exporting corporations purchasing bananas from Ecuadorian plantations, however, have fallen far short of fulfilling this responsibility. Similarly, the United States and the European Union, the two largest importers of Ecuadorian bananas, have failed to use their economic power to pressure for respect for the labor rights of banana workers, both young and old, in Ecuador.

The result is widespread labor rights abuses on Ecuador's banana plantations. Children labor for long hours in unsafe and unhealthy working conditions, often leaving school years before they reach the secondary level. Adults work in the same hazardous worksites, deterred from forming workers' organizations by fear of being fired—effectively denied the right to use this internationally sanctioned tool for demanding better working conditions. For many of these child and adult banana workers, laboring on banana plantations is a way of life. Unfortunately, so is the labor exploitation they suffer while the industry, Ecuador, and foreign markets benefit from the abuse.

APPENDIX A: METHODOLOGY

Human Rights Watch interviewed twenty-five adult and forty-five child banana workers, NGO representatives, government officials, union officials and labor activists, labor lawyers, child labor and children's rights experts, representatives of international organizations, and banana-exporting corporation officials in Ecuador from May 7, 2001 through May 27, 2001. In some cases, we also subsequently conducted follow-up telephone interviews from the United States.

Human Rights Watch interviewed government officials from a juvenile court, the Ministry of Labor, the Ecuadorian Institute of Social Security, and the Ministry of Agriculture between May 9 and May 23 in Quito and Guayaquil. Between May 7 and May 22, we spoke with a UNICEF official, several representatives of the National Institute for Children and Families, a child labor expert, NGO representatives, union leaders, and labor lawyers. Through the assistance of a local banana producer and the president of a small banana-producers association, Human Rights Watch visited several banana plantations on May 14 and May 15, and between May 14 and May 18, we spoke with plantation owners and administrators as well as representatives from small, medium, and large banana-producers associations. We interviewed representatives of UBESA, Dole's Ecuadorian subsidiary, on May 17, Favorita on May 21, and Bandecua, Del Monte's Ecuadorian subsidiary, Brundicorpi, Chiquita's Ecuadorian subsidiary, and Noboa on May 24. In July, we contacted the Brundicorpi official and another UBESA official by telephone from the United States.

Human Rights Watch also sent letters to the chief executive officers of all five banana-exporting corporations mentioned in this report, informing them of our investigation, inquiring as to their contractual relationships with certain Ecuadorian banana plantations on which workers we interviewed labored, and seeking information on their labor policies with respect to their Ecuadorian suppliers. We sent letters to Chiquita on July 13 and Favorita on July 15, and both corporations responded shortly thereafter. Letters were sent to Noboa on September 5 and October 5, but no response was ever received. Similarly, we sent letters to Del Monte on July 18, September 4, and September 5 and received no response. Human Rights Watch also sent letters to Dole on July 13, August 31, September 5, and September 8, to which Dole responded on October 8.

With the exception of a workshop for female banana workers on May 20, a meeting with the female banana worker organizing the workshop, and a Machala interview with a child worker, our access to banana workers was facilitated by a retired male banana worker, identified as Julio Gutiérrez in this report, who collaborates with a local agricultural workers' federation and with whom we spoke several times prior to traveling to Ecuador. On May 12 and May 27, Gutiérrez accompanied us to small villages in Naranjal and Balao, where he brought us from house to house to interview child and adult banana workers, the vast majority acquaintances of his and many of whom he had contacted on our behalf prior to our arrival. In some cases, while interviewing adults, we were informed of additional child workers in the villages, whom we later also interviewed. On May 19, Gutiérrez accompanied Human Rights Watch to a village in Balao, where we spent the day in a recreation center, surrounded by child banana workers. Gutiérrez had previously contacted parents in the village to explain the purpose of our visit and, upon our arrival, parents sent their children to the center to be interviewed. As word of our presence spread, more curious children flocked to the center, where we interviewed every child worker willing to speak with us. On May 26, Gutiérrez accompanied us to two other villages in Naranjal, where we interviewed adults and walked throughout one of the small communities inquiring as to whether child workers also lived in the village. In response, adults sent several children to speak with us, and one of the child workers gathered a number of his child worker acquaintances to be interviewed as well.

APPENDIX B: LETTERS TO CORPORATIONS

HUMAN RIGHTS WATCH

1630 Connecticut Avenue, N.W. Suite 500
Washington, DC 20009
Telephone: 202-612-4321
Facsimile: 202-612-4333
E-mail: hrwd
Website: http://www.hrw.org

AMERICAS DIVISION
José Miguel Vivanco
Executive Director
Joanne Mariner
Deputy Director
Joel Solomon
Research Director
Carol Pier
Researcher
Sebastian Brett
Robin Kirk
Research Associates
Tzeitel Cruz
Elizabeth Hollenback
Associates

ADVISORY COMMITTEE
Stephen L. Kass, *Chair*
Marina Pinto Kaufman
David Nachman
Vice Chairs
Roland Algrant
Peter D. Bell
Marcelo Bronstein
Paul Chevigny
Roberto Cuellar
Dorothy Cullman
Tom J. Farer
Alejandro Garro
Peter Hakim
Ronald G. Hellman
Bianca Jagger
Mark Kaplan
Margaret A. Lang
Kenneth Maxwell
Jocelyn McCalla
Bruce Rabb
Michael Shifter
George Soros
Julien Studley
Rose Styron
Javier Timerman
Horacio Verbitsky
José Zalaquett

HUMAN RIGHTS WATCH
Kenneth Roth
Executive Director
Michele Alexander
Development Director
Carroll Bogert
Communications Director
Reed Brody
Advocacy Director
Barbara Guglielmo
Finance Director
Lotte Leicht
Brussels Office Director
Michael McClintock
Deputy Program Director
Maria Pignataro Nielsen
Human Resources Director
Dinah PoKempner
General Counsel
Malcolm Smart
Program Director
Wilder Tayler
Legal and Policy Director
Joanna Weschler
UN Representative
Jonathan Fanton
Chair

Carl Linder
Chief Executive Officer
Chiquita Brands International, Inc.
250 East Fifth Street
Cincinnati, OH 45202
Via Fax: 513-579-2580

July 13, 2001

Dear Mr. Linder:

Human Rights Watch is preparing a report on child labor and freedom of association in the banana sector in Ecuador. Human Rights Watch is an independent, nongovernmental organization that since 1978 has conducted investigations of human rights abuses throughout the world.

Attached are questions regarding Chiquita's contractual relationships with specific Ecuadorean banana producers and plantations and Chiquita's general labor policies with respect to its Ecuadorean banana suppliers. We would appreciate your answers to these questions, which would be reflected in our report. In light of our publishing schedule, we would be grateful to receive your response within one month's time.

I also wish to request at your earliest convenience an interview with you or a Chiquita employee who is knowledgeable about labor practices on the plantations of Chiquita's suppliers in Ecuador.

Thank you very much. I look forward to hearing from you.

Sincerely,

Carol Pier
Labor Rights Researcher
Americas Division
Human Rights Watch

BRUSSELS HONG KONG LONDON LOS ANGELES MOSCOW NEW YORK RIO DE JANEIRO WASHINGTON

To: Chiquita Brands International, Inc.
From: Human Rights Watch
Date: July 13, 2001
Subject: Banana plantations in Ecuador producing for Chiquita

A. Chiquita Contractual Relationships

Human Rights Watch was informed that although Chiquita has not had long-standing contractual relationships, during the years indicated, with the plantations and producers listed below, Chiquita nonetheless has purchased bananas for export from them sporadically during these periods. We would be grateful if you would confirm this information.

> Cañas, owned by Vicente Ordoñez in the El Oro Province in the canton of Machala, from 1999 through 2001, and the following banana producers and plantations in Guayas Province: Balao Chico in the canton of Balao from 1995 through 2001; Las Fincas, comprised of San Fernando, San Alejandro, San Gabriel, and San José, in the canton of Balao from 1995 through 2001; Italia in the canton of Balao from 1995 through 2001; Colón in the canton of Balao from 1995 through 2001; Recreo in the canton of Naranjal from 2000 through 2001; San Carlos in the canton of Balao from 1999 through 2001; Santa Carla in the canton of Balao from 1997 through 2001; Flor María of Sociedad Predio Rústico Agrícola Italia in the canton of Balao from 1997 through 2001; Guabital in the canton of Balao from 1998 through 2001; Alamos-Rey Rancho in the canton of Naranjal from 1995 through 2001; Predio Rústico La Rural, C.A., in the canton of Balao from 1999 through 2001.

We would also welcome the names and locations of the producers and plantations in Ecuador that are among Chiquita's principal suppliers and with which Chiquita has had contractual relationships between 1995 and May 2001.

B. Chiquita Labor Practices

We would appreciate information about the policies Chiquita has adopted regarding respect for labor rights on the plantations from which it purchases bananas for export—both those with which it has standing contractual relationships and those from which it purchases bananas on an irregular basis.

Specifically, we would welcome your responses to the following questions:

1. Does Chiquita impose any age restrictions on workers employed on these plantations? Are there age restrictions for the performance of

certain types of tasks or for working under certain conditions? What steps does Chiquita take to ensure compliance with those restrictions?
2. Does Chiquita have a policy with respect to the use of temporary workers and subcontractors and the duration of their contracts on these plantations?
3. What steps does Chiquita take to ensure that the right to freedom of association, including the right to unionize, is respected on these plantations?
4. Does Chiquita monitor, on an ongoing basis, labor rights conditions on the Ecuadorean plantations from which it purchases bananas for export? Has Chiquita conducted any labor rights monitoring or inspections of the above-listed Ecuadorean banana producers and plantations?

HUMAN RIGHTS WATCH

1630 Connecticut Avenue, N.W. Suite 500
Washington, DC 20009
Telephone: 202-612-4321
Facsimile: 202-612-4333
E-mail: hrwd
Website: http://www.hrw.org

AMERICAS DIVISION
José Miguel Vivanco
Executive Director
Joanne Mariner
Deputy Director
Joel Solomon
Research Director
Carol Pier
Researcher
Sebastian Brett
Robin Kirk
Research Associates
Tzeitel Cruz
Elizabeth Hollenback
Associates

ADVISORY COMMITTEE
Stephen L. Kass, *Chair*
Marina Pinto Kaufman
David Nachman
Vice Chairs
Roland Algrant
Peter D. Bell
Marcelo Bronstein
Paul Chevigny
Roberto Cuellar
Dorothy Cullman
Tom J. Farer
Alejandro Garro
Peter Hakim
Ronald G. Hellman
Bianca Jagger
Mark Kaplan
Margaret A. Lang
Kenneth Maxwell
Jocelyn McCalla
Bruce Rabb
Michael Shifter
George Soros
Julien Studley
Rose Styron
Javier Timerman
Horacio Verbitsky
José Zalaquett

HUMAN RIGHTS WATCH
Kenneth Roth
Executive Director
Michele Alexander
Development Director
Carroll Bogert
Communications Director
Reed Brody
Advocacy Director
Barbara Guglielmo
Finance Director
Lotte Leicht
Brussels Office Director
Michael McClintock
Deputy Program Director
Maria Pignataro Nielsen
Human Resources Director
Dinah PoKempner
General Counsel
Malcolm Smart
Program Director
Wilder Tayler
Legal and Policy Director
Joanna Weschler
UN Representative
Jonathan Fanton
Chair

Mohammad Abu-Ghazaleh
Chief Executive Officer
Del Monte Fresh Produce Company
800 Douglas Road
North Tower, 12th Floor
Coral Gables, FL 33134
Via Fax: 305-520-8495

July 18, 2001

Dear Mr. Abu-Ghazaleh:

Human Rights Watch is preparing a report on child labor and freedom of association in the banana sector in Ecuador. Human Rights Watch is an independent, nongovernmental organization that since 1978 has conducted investigations of human rights abuses throughout the world.

Attached are questions regarding Del Monte's contractual relationships with specific Ecuadorean banana producers and plantations and Del Monte's general labor policies with respect to its Ecuadorean banana suppliers. We would appreciate your answers to these questions, which would be reflected in our report. In light of our publishing schedule, we would be grateful to receive your response within one month's time.

I also wish to request at your earliest convenience an interview with you or a Del Monte employee who is knowledgeable about labor practices on the plantations of Del Monte's suppliers in Ecuador.

Thank you very much. I look forward to hearing from you.

Sincerely,

Carol Pier
Labor Rights Researcher
Americas Division
Human Rights Watch

BRUSSELS HONG KONG LONDON LOS ANGELES MOSCOW NEW YORK RIO DE JANEIRO WASHINGTON

To: Del Monte Fresh Produce Company
From: Human Rights Watch
Date: July 18, 2001
Subject: Banana plantations in Ecuador producing for Del Monte

A.   Del Monte Contractual Relationships

Human Rights Watch was informed that the plantations and producers listed below are among Del Monte's principal Ecuadorean banana suppliers and were producing primarily for Del Monte during the years stated or that Del Monte purchased significant quantities of bananas from them on a regular basis during these periods. We would be grateful if you would confirm this information and state when your contractual relationship with each producer and plantation began and whether the relationship still existed as of May 2001 or, if no standing contractual relationship existed, when you began to purchase significant quantities of bananas from these producers and plantations and whether you continue to do so.

> Plantations and producers in Guayas Province: Santa Carla in the canton of Balao from 1997 through 2001; Fátima in the canton of Naranjal from 1995 through 2001; Guabital in the canton of Balao from 1998 through 2001; and San Miguel in the canton of Naranjal from 2000 through 2001.

Human Rights Watch was also informed that although Del Monte has not had long-standing contractual relationships, during the years indicated, with the plantations and producers listed below, Del Monte nonetheless has purchased bananas for export from them sporadically during these periods. We would be grateful if you would confirm this information as well.

> Cañas, owned by Vicente Ordoñez, from 1999 through 2001, and Cañas, owned by Victor Moreno, in 1997, both in the province of El Oro in the canton of Machala, and the following group of banana producers and plantations in the Guayas Province: Recreo in the canton of Naranjal from 2000 through 2001; Pachina in the canton of Balao in 2001; Balao Chico in the canton of Balao from 1995 through 2001; Las Fincas, comprised of San Fernando, San Alejandro, San Gabriel, and San José, in the canton of Balao from 1995 through 2001; San José of Parazul, S.A., in the canton of Balao from 1999 through 2001; Italia in the canton of Balao from 1995 through 2001; Colón in the canton of Balao from 1995 through 2001; San Carlos in the canton of Balao from 1999 through 2001; Alamos-Rey Rancho in the canton of Naranjal from 1995 through 2001; and Flor María of Sociedad Predio Rústico Agrícola Italia in the canton of Balao from 1997 through 2001.

We would also welcome the names and locations of the other producers and plantations in Ecuador that are among Del Monte's principal suppliers and with which Del Monte has had contractual relationships between 1995 and May 2001.

B.   Del Monte Labor Practices

We would appreciate information about the policies Del Monte has adopted regarding respect for labor rights on the plantations from which it purchases bananas for export—both those with which it has standing contractual relationships and those from which it purchases bananas on an irregular basis.

Specifically, we would welcome your responses to the following questions:

1. Does Del Monte impose any age restrictions on workers employed on these plantations? Are there age restrictions for the performance of certain types of tasks or for working under certain conditions? What steps does Del Monte take to ensure compliance with those restrictions?
2. Does Del Monte have a policy with respect to the use of temporary workers and subcontractors and the duration of their contracts on these plantations?
3. What steps does Del Monte take to ensure that the right to freedom of association, including the right to unionize, is respected on these plantations?
4. Does Del Monte monitor, on an ongoing basis, labor rights conditions on the Ecuadorean plantations from which it purchases bananas for export? Has Del Monte conducted any labor rights monitoring or inspections of the above-listed Ecuadorean banana producers and plantations?

HUMAN RIGHTS WATCH

1630 Connecticut Avenue, N.W. Suite 500
Washington, DC 20009
Telephone: 202-612-4321
Facsimile: 202-612-4333
E-mail: hrwd
Website: http://www.hrw.org

AMERICAS DIVISION
José Miguel Vivanco
Executive Director
Joanne Mariner
Deputy Director
Joel Solomon
Research Director
Carol Pier
Researcher
Sebastian Brett
Robin Kirk
Research Associates
Tzeitel Cruz
Elizabeth Hollenback
Associates

ADVISORY COMMITTEE
Stephen L. Kass, *Chair*
Marina Pinto Kaufman
David Nachman
Vice Chairs
Roland Algrant
Peter D. Bell
Marcelo Bronstein
Paul Chevigny
Roberto Cuellar
Dorothy Cullman
Tom J. Farer
Alejandro Garro
Peter Hakim
Ronald G. Hellman
Bianca Jagger
Mark Kaplan
Margaret A. Lang
Kenneth Maxwell
Jocelyn McCalla
Bruce Rabb
Michael Shifter
George Soros
Julien Studley
Rose Styron
Javier Timerman
Horacio Verbitsky
José Zalaquett

HUMAN RIGHTS WATCH
Kenneth Roth
Executive Director
Michele Alexander
Development Director
Carroll Bogert
Communications Director
Reed Brody
Advocacy Director
Barbara Guglielmo
Finance Director
Lotte Leicht
Brussels Office Director
Michael McClintock
Deputy Program Director
Maria Pignataro Nielsen
Human Resources Director
Dinah PoKempner
General Counsel
Malcolm Smart
Program Director
Wilder Tayler
Legal and Policy Director
Joanna Weschler
UN Representative
Jonathan Fanton
Chair

David H. Murdock
Chief Executive Officer
Dole Food Company, Inc.
One Dole Drive
Westlake Village, CA 91362-7300
Via Fax: 818-874-4893

July 13, 2001

Dear Mr. Murdock:

Human Rights Watch is preparing a report on child labor and freedom of association in the banana sector in Ecuador. Human Rights Watch is an independent, nongovernmental organization that since 1978 has conducted investigations of human rights abuses throughout the world.

Attached are questions regarding Dole's contractual relationships with specific Ecuadorean banana producers and plantations and Dole's general labor policies with respect to its Ecuadorean banana suppliers. We would appreciate your answers to these questions, which would be reflected in our report. In light of our publishing schedule, we would be grateful to receive your response within one month's time.

I also wish to request at your earliest convenience an interview with you or a Dole employee who is knowledgeable about labor practices on the plantations of Dole's suppliers in Ecuador.

Thank you very much. I look forward to hearing from you.

Sincerely,

Carol Pier
Labor Rights Researcher
Americas Division
Human Rights Watch

BRUSSELS HONG KONG LONDON LOS ANGELES MOSCOW NEW YORK RIO DE JANEIRO WASHINGTON

To: Dole Food Company, Inc.
From: Human Rights Watch
Date: July 13, 2001
Subject: Banana plantations in Ecuador producing for Dole

A. Dole Contractual Relationships

Human Rights Watch was informed that the plantations and producers listed below are among Dole's approximately 300 principal Ecuadorean banana suppliers and were producing primarily for Dole during the years stated. We would be grateful if you would confirm this information and state when your contractual relationship with each producer and plantation began and whether the relationship still existed as of May 2001.

> Plantations and producers in Guayas Province: Recreo in the canton of Naranjal from 2000 through 2001; Pachina in the canton of Balao in 2001; Pitufina, S.A., in the canton of Balao from 1998 through 2001; Porvenir in the canton of Balao from 1995 through 2001; Luz Belén in the canton of Balao from 1995 through 2001; Balao Chico in the canton of Balao from 1995 through 2001; La María of Frutos Bellos, C.A., in the canton of Balao from 1995 through 2001; Las Fincas, comprised of San Fernando, San Alejandro, San Gabriel, and San José, in the canton of Balao from 1995 through 2001; San José of Krapp, S.A., in the canton of Balao in 1999; San José of Parazul, S.A., in the canton of Balao from 1999 through 2001; Italia in the canton of Balao from 1995 through 2001; "Chanique" in the canton of Balao from 1999 through 2001; San Vicente in the canton of Balao in 1999; Predio Rústico La Rural, C.A., in the canton of Balao from 1999 through 2001; and El Gran Chaparral in the canton of Balao from 1999 through 2000.

Human Rights Watch was also informed that although Dole has not had long-standing contractual relationships, during the years indicated, with the plantations and producers listed below, Dole nonetheless has purchased bananas for export from them sporadically during these periods. We would be grateful if you would confirm this information as well.

> Cañas, owned by Vicente Ordoñez in the El Oro Province in the canton of Machala, from 1999 through 2001, and the following banana producers and plantations in Guayas Province: Colón in the canton of Balao from 1995 through 2001; Paladines in the canton of Balao from 1999 through 2001; San Francisco in the canton of Balao from 1995 through 2001; San Carlos in the canton of Balao from 1999 through 2001; Flor María of Sociedad Predio Rústico Agrícola Italia in the canton of Balao from 1997 through 2001; and Alamos-Rey Rancho in the canton of Naranjal from 1995 through 2001.

We would also welcome the names and locations of the other producers and plantations in Ecuador that are among Dole's approximately 300 principal suppliers and with which Dole has had contractual relationships between 1995 and May 2001.

B.   Dole Labor Practices

We would appreciate information about the policies Dole has adopted regarding respect for labor rights on the plantations from which it purchases bananas for export—both those with which it has standing contractual relationships and those from which it purchases bananas on an irregular basis.

Specifically, we would welcome your responses to the following questions:

1. Does Dole impose any age restrictions on workers employed on these plantations? Are there age restrictions for the performance of certain types of tasks or for working under certain conditions? What steps does Dole take to ensure compliance with those restrictions?
2. Does Dole have a policy with respect to the use of temporary workers and subcontractors and the duration of their contracts on these plantations?
3. What steps does Dole take to ensure that the right to freedom of association, including the right to unionize, is respected on these plantations?
4. Does Dole monitor, on an ongoing basis, labor rights conditions on the Ecuadorean plantations from which it purchases bananas for export? Has Dole conducted any labor rights monitoring or inspections of the above-listed Ecuadorean banana producers and plantations?

HUMAN RIGHTS WATCH

1630 Connecticut Avenue, N.W. Suite 500
Washington, DC 20009
Telephone: 202-612-4321
Facsimile: 202-612-4333
E-mail: hrwdc@hrw.org
Website:http://www.hrw.org

AMERICAS DIVISION
José Miguel Vivanco
Executive Director
Joanne Mariner
Deputy Director
Joel Solomon
Research Director
Carol Pier
Researcher
Sebastian Brett
Robin Kirk
Research Associates
Tzeitel Cruz
Elizabeth Hollenback
Associates
ADVISORY COMMITTEE
Stephen L. Kass, *Chair*
Marina Pinto Kaufman
David Nachman
Vice Chairs
Roland Algrant
Peter D. Bell
Marcelo Bronstein
Paul Chevigny
Roberto Cuellar
Dorothy Cullman
Tom J. Farer
Alejandro Garro
Peter Hakim
Ronald G. Hellman
Bianca Jagger
Mark Kaplan
Margaret A. Lang
Kenneth Maxwell
Jocelyn McCalla
Bruce Rabb
Michael Shifter
George Soros
Julien Studley
Rose Styron
Javier Timerman
Horacio Verbitsky
José Zalaquett

HUMAN RIGHTS WATCH
Kenneth Roth
Executive Director
Michele Alexander
Development Director
Carroll Bogert
Communications Director
Reed Brody
Advocacy Director
Barbara Guglielmo
Finance Director
Lotte Leicht
Brussels Office Director
Michael McClintock
Deputy Program Director
Maria Pignataro Nielsen
Human Resources Director
Dinah PoKempner
General Counsel
Malcolm Smart
Program Director
Wilder Tayler
Legal and Policy Director
Joanna Weschler
UN Representative
Jonathan Fanton
Chair

Dr. Segundo Wong Mayorga
Executive President
Favorita Fruit Company
Avenida Carlos Julio Arosemena Km. 1 ½ Mz. 001 solar 41(2),
    frente al Centro Comercial Albán Borja
Guayaquil, Ecuador
Via Fax: 011-593-4208-660 or 011-593-4208-661

July 13, 2001

Dear Dr. Wong:

Human Rights Watch is preparing a report on child labor and freedom of association in the banana sector in Ecuador. Human Rights Watch is an independent, nongovernmental organization that since 1978 has conducted investigations of human rights abuses throughout the world.

Attached are questions regarding Favorita's contractual relationships with specific Ecuadorean banana producers and plantations and Favorita's general labor policies with respect to its Ecuadorean banana suppliers. We would appreciate your answers to these questions, which would be reflected in our report. In light of our publishing schedule, we would be grateful to receive your response within one month's time.

I also wish to request at your earliest convenience an interview with you or a Favorita employee who is knowledgeable about labor practices on the plantations of Favorita's suppliers in Ecuador.

Thank you very much. I look forward to hearing from you.

Sincerely,

Carol Pier
Labor Rights Researcher
Americas Division
Human Rights Watch

BRUSSELS   HONG KONG   LONDON   LOS ANGELES   MOSCOW   NEW YORK   RIO DE JANEIRO   WASHINGTON

To: Favorita Fruit Company
From: Human Rights Watch
Date: July 13, 2001
Subject: Banana plantations in Ecuador producing for Favorita

A. Favorita Contractual Relationships

Human Rights Watch was informed that La Juanita in the canton of Balao in the province of Guayas, from 1995 through 2001, was among Favorita's principal Ecuadorean banana suppliers and was producing primarily for Favorita during the years stated or that Favorita purchased significant quantities of bananas from La Juanita on a regular basis during that period. We would be grateful if you would confirm this information and state when your contractual relationship with La Juanita began and whether the relationship still existed as of May 2001 or, if no standing contractual relationship existed, when you began to purchase significant quantities of bananas from La Juanita and whether you continue to do so.

Human Rights Watch was also informed that although Favorita has not had long-standing contractual relationships, during the years indicated, with the plantations and producers listed below, Favorita nonetheless has purchased bananas for export from them sporadically during these periods. We would be grateful if you would confirm this information as well.

> Plantations and producers in Guayas Province: Balao Chico in the canton of Balao from 1995 through 2001; and Italia in the canton of Balao from 1995 through 2001.

We would also welcome the names and locations of the other producers and plantations in Ecuador that are among Favorita's principal suppliers and with which Favorita has had contractual relationships between 1995 and May 2001.

B. Favorita Labor Practices

We would appreciate information about the policies Favorita has adopted regarding respect for labor rights on the plantations from which it purchases bananas for export—both those with which it has standing contractual relationships and those from which it purchases bananas on an irregular basis.

Specifically, we would welcome your responses to the following questions:

1. Does Favorita impose any age restrictions on workers employed on these plantations? Are there age restrictions for the performance of certain types of tasks or for working under certain conditions? What steps does Favorita take to ensure compliance with those restrictions?

2. Does Favorita have a policy with respect to the use of temporary workers and subcontractors and the duration of their contracts on these plantations?
3. What steps does Favorita take to ensure that the right to freedom of association, including the right to unionize, is respected on these plantations?
4. Does Favorita monitor, on an ongoing basis, labor rights conditions on the Ecuadorean plantations from which it purchases bananas for export? Has Favorita conducted any labor rights monitoring or inspections of the above-listed Ecuadorean banana producers and plantations?

HUMAN RIGHTS WATCH

1630 Connecticut Avenue, N.W. Suite 500
Washington, DC 20009
Telephone: 202-612-4321
Facsimile: 202-612-4333
E-mail: hrwdc
Website: http://www.hrw.org

AMERICAS DIVISION
José Miguel Vivanco
Executive Director
Joanne Mariner
Deputy Director
Joel Solomon
Research Director
Carol Pier
Researcher
Sebastian Brett
Robin Kirk
Research Associates
Tzeitel Cruz
Elizabeth Hollenback
Associates

ADVISORY COMMITTEE
Stephen L. Kass, *Chair*
Marina Pinto Kaufman
David Nachman
Vice Chairs
Roland Algrant
Peter D. Bell
Marcelo Bronstein
Paul Chevigny
Roberto Cuellar
Dorothy Cullman
Tom J. Farer
Alejandro Garro
Peter Hakim
Ronald G. Hellman
Bianca Jagger
Mark Kaplan
Margaret A. Lang
Kenneth Maxwell
Jocelyn McCalla
Bruce Rabb
Michael Shifter
George Soros
Julien Studley
Rose Styron
Javier Timerman
Horacio Verbitsky
José Zalaquett

HUMAN RIGHTS WATCH
Kenneth Roth
Executive Director
Michele Alexander
Development Director
Carroll Bogert
Communications Director
Reed Brody
Advocacy Director
Barbara Guglielmo
Finance Director
Lotte Leicht
Brussels Office Director
Michael McClintock
Deputy Program Director
Maria Pignataro Nielsen
Human Resources Director
Dinah PoKempner
General Counsel
Malcolm Smart
Program Director
Wilder Tayler
Legal and Policy Director
Joanna Weschler
UN Representative
Jonathan Fanton
Chair

Alvaro Noboa
Chief Executive Officer
Exportadora Bananera Noboa, S.A.
El Oro 1010 y La Ría
Guayaquil, Ecuador
Via Fax: 593-42-445138

September 5, 2001

Dear Mr. Noboa:

Human Rights Watch is preparing a report on child labor and freedom of association in the banana sector in Ecuador. Human Rights Watch is an independent, nongovernmental organization that since 1978 has conducted investigations of human rights abuses throughout the world.

On July 13, 2001, I faxed and mailed the attached questions to Mr. Carlos Aguirre, head of your foreign office in Staten Island, New York. To date, he has not responded to the inquiries. When I contacted his office by telephone last week, I was instructed that the letter, instead, should be directed to you.

Attached are questions regarding Noboa's contractual relationships with specific Ecuadorean banana producers and plantations and Noboa's general labor policies with respect to its Ecuadorean banana suppliers. We would appreciate your answers to these questions, which would be reflected in our report. In light of our publishing schedule, we would be grateful to receive your response as soon as possible.

I also wish to request at your earliest convenience an interview with you or a Noboa employee who is knowledgeable about labor practices on the plantations of Noboa's suppliers in Ecuador.

Thank you very much. I look forward to hearing from you.

Sincerely,

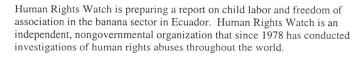

Carol Pier
Labor Rights Researcher
Americas Division
Human Rights Watch

To: Exportadora Bananera Noboa, S.A.
From: Human Rights Watch
Date: July 13, 2001
Subject: Banana plantations in Ecuador producing for Noboa

A.   Noboa Contractual Relationships

Human Rights Watch was informed that the plantations and producers listed below are among Noboa's principal Ecuadorean banana suppliers and were producing primarily for Noboa during the years stated and that Noboa directly owned Alamos-Rey Rancho during the period listed. We would be grateful if you would confirm this information and state when your contractual relationship with each producer and plantation began and whether the relationship still existed as of May 2001 and when Noboa obtained ownership of Alamos-Rey Rancho and whether Noboa continued to own the plantation as of May 2001.

> Plantations and producers in Guayas Province: Paladines in the canton of Balao from 1999 through 2001; San Carlos in the canton of Balao from 1999 through 2001; San Francisco in the canton of Balao from 1995 through 2001; Recreo #1 and Recreo #3 in the canton of Naranjal from 1999 through 2001; Flor María of Sociedad Predio Rústico Agrícola Italia in the canton of Balao from 1997 through 2001; Colón in the canton of Balao from 1995 through 2001; and Alamos-Rey Rancho in the canton of Naranjal from 1995 through 2001.

Human Rights Watch was also informed that although Noboa has not had long-standing contractual relationships, during the years indicated, with the plantations and producers listed below, Noboa nonetheless has purchased bananas for export from them sporadically during these periods. We would be grateful if you would confirm this information as well.

> Cañas, owned by Vicente Ordoñez in the El Oro Province in the canton of Machala, from 1999 through 2001, and the following banana producers and plantations in Guayas Province: Pachina in the canton of Balao in 2001; Santa Carla in the canton of Balao from 1997 through 2001; Guabital in the canton of Balao from 1998 through 2001; San Miguel in the canton of Naranjal from 2000 through 2001; Luz Belén in the canton of Balao from 1995 through 2001; Balao Chico in the canton of Balao from 1995 through 2001; La María of Frutos Bellos, C.A., in the canton of Balao from 1995 through 2001; and Italia in the canton of Balao from 1995 through 2001.

We would also welcome the names and locations of the other producers and plantations in Ecuador that are among Noboa's principal suppliers and with which Noboa has had contractual relationships between 1995 and May 2001.

B.   Noboa Labor Practices

We would appreciate information about the policies Noboa has adopted regarding respect for labor rights on the plantations from which it purchases bananas for export—both those with which it has standing contractual relationships and those from which it purchases bananas on an irregular basis.

Specifically, we would welcome your responses to the following questions:

1. Does Noboa impose any age restrictions on workers employed on these plantations? Are there age restrictions for the performance of certain types of tasks or for working under certain conditions? What steps does Noboa take to ensure compliance with those restrictions?
2. Does Noboa have a policy with respect to the use of temporary workers and subcontractors and the duration of their contracts on these plantations?
3. What steps does Noboa take to ensure that the right to freedom of association, including the right to unionize, is respected on these plantations?
4. Does Noboa monitor, on an ongoing basis, labor rights conditions on the Ecuadorean plantations from which it purchases bananas for export? Has Noboa conducted any labor rights monitoring or inspections of the above-listed Ecuadorean banana producers and plantations?

APPENDIX C: RESPONSE LETTERS FROM CORPORATIONS

July 25, 2001

Carol Pier
Labor Rights Researcher
Americas Division
Human Rights Watch
1630 Connecticut Avenue N.W. Suite 500
Washington, DC 20009

Dear Ms. Pier:

We welcome the interest of Human Rights Watch in labor conditions in the banana industry. We are pleased to acknowledge receipt of your letter of July 13, 2001 to Mr. Carl Lindner regarding Chiquita's contractual relationships with certain Ecuadorean banana farms and the Company's general labor policies.

We intend to fully reply to your letter, and we anticipate doing so by your requested reply date of August 13, 2001.

While we are developing a complete reply to your inquiry, you may be interested to read the enclosed materials.

1) In May 2000, we adopted as Company policy our "Code of Conduct ... Living by our Core Values." This document reflects Chiquita's commitment to leading standards of socially responsible, ethical and legal business conduct. You will note that we have incorporated into our Code the labor standard SA8000, which was developed by Social Accountability International, an independent NGO, through an extensive process of consultation and dialogue with a variety of stakeholders. Through this Code, we have:
   a) Agreed to respect the principles of the fundamental labor conventions of the International Labor Organization, the UN Convention on the Rights of the Child, and the Universal Declaration of Human Rights; and
   b) communicated our ultimate goal of directing "all of our business to suppliers that demonstrate their compliance with the Social Responsibilities included in our Code of Conduct, and that operate in an ethical and lawful manner."

2) In June 2001, we signed an agreement with COLSIBA and the International Union of Foodworkers (IUF) "On Freedom of Association, Minimum Labour Standards, and Employment in Latin American Banana Operations." COLSIBA is a regional affiliation of Latin American banana labor unions, through which most of our employees are represented in collective bargaining with the Company. The IUF, based in Geneva, is a highly respected international labor union secretariat with significant membership in the food and agriculture sectors. Through this agreement with unions, Chiquita reaffirmed its commitment to adhere to the core ILO Conventions in its Latin American banana operations, and it established a Review Committee that will meet regularly to address any issues of concern that may arise about Chiquita's labor practices.

If you have not done so already, you may also want to contact the following NGO and labor union leaders who are familiar with this recent IUF/COLSIBA/Chiquita agreement as well as with Chiquita's practices and approach to labor issues. Mr. Stephen Coats of U.S./LEAP has just himself returned from a recent trip to Ecuador to explore issues of concern similar to your own.

Ron Oswald
General Secretary
IUF - Intl Union of Food, Agricultural, Hotel, Restaurant, Catering, Tobacco and Allied Workers' Associations
CH-1213 Geneve/Petit-Lancy 2
Rampe du Pont-Rouge 8
Switzerland

Work: +41 22 793 22 33
Fax: +41 22 793 22 38
E-Mail: ron.oswald@iuf.org

Stephen Coats
Executive Director
U.S. Labor Education in the Americas
1449 W. Fargo
Chicago, IL 60626

Work: 773 262 6502
Fax: 773 262 6602
E-Mail: usglep@igc.org

German Zepeda
Coordinator, COLSIBA
Honduras

Work: 504 668 1736
Fax: (same; telephone first)
E-Mail: cosibah@publinet.hn / cosibah@sigmanet.hn

If you have questions beyond the scope of those listed in your July 13 letter, it would be most convenient if you could please send them in writing to me, and I will work to ensure that you receive the most complete and helpful reply possible.

Yours truly,

Jeffrey M. Zalla
Corporate Responsibility Officer

August 28, 2001

Carol Pier
Labor Rights Researcher
Americas Division
Human Rights Watch
1630 Connecticut Avenue N.W. Suite 500
Washington, DC 20009

Dear Ms. Pier:

This follows my earlier letter of July 25, 2001 about Chiquita's labor policies, our relationships with banana labor unions, and organizations familiar with our performance in the areas of working conditions and labor rights.

Allow me to address both the specific questions in your letter of July 13, 2001 about Chiquita's labor practices in Ecuador and also, more generally, the standards Chiquita applies to its purchases from independent banana growers regarding social and environmental performance.

You are correct that in recent years Chiquita has not had any long-term contracts for the purchase of fruit from Ecuador. However, each year we have purchased varying amounts of fruit in Ecuador, both to manage seasonal variations in supply and demand and in response to natural disasters that have reduced the supply available from our owned farms and those of independent producers in other countries.

We have reviewed the farms that have supplied Chiquita fruit in recent years and can confirm that, of the 15 farms identified in your letter, none supplied Chiquita any fruit in 1996 and only two did so between 1997 and 1999, in small quantities, as shown in the table below.

Farm	Province	Cantón	Owner	Boxes
Italia	Guayas	Balao	Sociedad Predio Rústico Agroitalia	1997: 19,544 1998: 13,874 1999: 12,607
Santa Carla	Guayas	Balao	Agricola Santa Carla	1999: 122,184

The fruit supplied by the farm Santa Clara represented less than 0.7% of the 18 million boxes Chiquita shipped from Ecuador in 1999, when we purchased substantial volumes to replace fruit lost due to Hurricane Mitch, which destroyed many of our farms in Honduras and Guatemala in late 1998.

Importantly, none of the farms identified in your letter supplied Chiquita any fruit during the year 2000, when we exported fewer than six million boxes, or in 2001, in which we have exported just over five million boxes through the end of June.

In recent years we have purchased virtually all of our fruit from Ecuador through the Favorita Fruit Company, which supplies much of that fruit from the farms of Reybancorp (also owned by the Wong family) and the balance from its own independent growers.

All of the Reybancorp farms, or over 7,000 hectares of banana production, are certified to the environmental and social standards of the Rainforest Alliance's Better Banana Project, which includes standards on "Fair Treatment and Good Conditions for Workers." *(For more information, see www.rainforest-alliance.org or contact Mr. Chris Wille, Director, Conservation Agriculture Network, Rainforest Alliance, cwille@racsa.co.cr.)*

Because we believe that the Wong group is the most responsible grower operating in Ecuador, for several years we have stipulated in our contracts with them that the Chiquita fruit they provide must, as much as possible, be supplied from these certified farms. In 2000 and year-to-date June 2001, 56% and 63%, respectively, of the fruit supplied to Chiquita from the Wongs came from these certified farms. (Even more fruit would come from these farms were it not for the fact that our ships must typically be loaded within 2 days while a normal farm harvest occurs over 5 days.)

Chiquita's Code of Conduct and our recent agreement with COLSIBA and the IUF, both of which I provided earlier, address Chiquita's labor rights policies and our application of those policies to independent growers.

Social and environmental responsibility issues were important in our selection of, and have helped to frame our ongoing relationship with, the Wong group as our principal banana suppliers in Ecuador. Chiquita's achievement of Better Banana Project certification on 100% of its owned farms in Latin America encouraged the Wong group toward the same accomplishment. The Wong group has chosen to follow Chiquita's own strict policies regarding the application of pesticides. The Wongs provide generous pay and benefits when compared to the rest of the industry in Ecuador.

In addition to receiving assurance from the independent Better Banana Project audits, since 1999 Chiquita has also conducted its own periodic sample assessments of the social and environmental performance of the Wongs' farms and those of its suppliers in Ecuador. Discussions of the challenges and opportunities to improve social and environmental performance are part of the ongoing, normal dialogue between leaders of both companies. For example, in June 2001, leaders of both firms discussed whether it would be prudent for the Wong group to adopt the SA8000 labor standard for its banana operations, as Chiquita has done in its own Code of Conduct.

More information about the challenges Ecuador presents is included in the enclosed case study entitled "Standards for Independent Banana Growers," which will be included in the 2000 Corporate Responsibility Report that we expect to release publicly in mid-September. The case study outlines the issues as well as our efforts to lead improved grower and industry performance through assessments, contracts and certification programs. I will be sure that you also receive a copy of the full Report when it is released.

We appreciate the efforts of Human Rights Watch to foster greater respect for worker rights in the banana industry. We appreciate the opportunity to respond to your questions, and if we may be of further assistance, we would be pleased to do so.

Yours truly,

Jeffrey M. Zalla
Corporate Responsibility Officer

cc: Mr. Ricardo Flores

 Food Company, Inc.
One Dole Drive, Westlake Village, CA 91362-7300 • Phone (818) 879-6812 • Fax (818) 879-6602

Freya Maneki
Director, Corporate Communications & Shareholder Relations
and Assistant Corporate Secretary

Via Facsimile 202-612-4333

October 8, 2001

Carol Pier
Labor rights Researcher
Americas Division
Human Rights Watch
1630 Connecticut Avenue, N.W., Suite 500
Washington, DC 20009

Dear Ms. Pier:

Dole Food Company, Inc. has been recognized internationally as a company that is socially responsible, ethical and committed to sound environmental practices. Dole has received numerous awards, including being:

- among the top ten companies ranked overall in environmental and social responsibility by the Council on Economic Priorities

- honored with the first-ever ethical workplace award from Social Accountability International

- ranked by Fortune Magazine as one of America's best companies for minorities

- ranked by Innovest as fourth out of 23 companies studied in the food industry and first among United States companies in environmental health and safety in August 2000

The Latin America Quality Institute gave Dole a special award for company excellence in environmental management.

The following information is being provided to the Human Rights Watch in response to your recent inquiry to Dole regarding certain of Dole's practices in Ecuador.

A. Dole Contractual Relationships

Dole's contractual relationship with its suppliers, the plantations and/or producers with whom Dole has or may have had a relationship is proprietary business information, which Dole does not publicly disclose.

B. Dole Labor Practices

1. Does Dole impose any age restrictions on workers employed on these plantations? Are there age restrictions for the performance of certain types of tasks or for working under certain conditions? What steps does Dole take to ensure compliance with those restrictions?

   It is Dole's policy to comply with all applicable regulations and laws of any country in which it or its affiliates operate, including those relating to labor practices. Dole does not employ minors (under 18 years of age). Four percent of Ubesa's labor force is between the ages of 19 and 21, 44% between 22 and 30, and 52% are over 30.

   Dole audits its suppliers for compliance in the areas of: quality, health, hygiene, safety and environmental performance. Dole's operations, including its internal audits, are certified to ISO 14001 and ISO 9002. Ubesa was the first company in Ecuador certified to ISO 14001 and ISO 9002.

2. Does Dole have a policy with respect to the use of temporary workers and subcontractors and the duration of their contracts on these plantations?

   Dole prefers to use permanent, full-time workers. However, due to the nature of the agricultural business, workers are hired for a limited time to perform specific tasks.

3. What steps does Dole take to ensure that the right to freedom of association, including the right to unionize, is respected on these plantations?

   It is Dole's policy to comply with all applicable regulations and laws of any country in which it or its affiliates operate, including the right to collective bargaining.

4. Does Dole monitor, on an ongoing basis, labor rights conditions on the Ecuadorian plantations from which it purchases bananas for export? Has Dole conducted any labor rights monitoring or inspections of the above-listed Ecuadorian banana producers and plantations?

As mentioned in the response to question one, Dole audits its suppliers in a number of areas, including labor rights. Dole will not comment on monitoring or inspections of a specific producer or plantation.

Thank you for the opportunity to respond to your questions.

Very truly yours,

FAVORITA
FRUIT COMPANY

Guayaquil, July 17, 2001

Mr.
CAROL PIER
Labor Rights Researcher
Human Rights Watch
Washington DC

Dear Mr. Carol:

We are pleased to respond to your queries of July 13th, 2001.

FAVORITA FRUIT Co. Ltd. is a British Virgin Islands holding company and does not have offices or representation in Ecuador.

However, Favorita has equity interests in the following Ecuadorean companies: REYBANPAC, REY BANANO DEL PACIFICO C.A. y AGRICOLA BANANERA REYBANCORP ABR S.A. which produce and sell fruit locally and internationally.

The farm referenced in your letter, La Juanita, supposedly located in Balao parish and is not owned directly or indirectly by Favorita Fruit Co Ltd or any of its subsdiaries, nor is its fruit purchased by Favorita subsidiaries.

We do not know its exact location or its owner.

The labor rights of workers hired to perform farm work in Reybanpac or Reybancorp farms are strictly within social and economic legislation in force in Ecuador, including the labor code. In particular, rights related to compensation, social benefits and ages are strictly adhered to and closely monitored by management..

In addition, the aforementioned farms are certified in environmental and social management. Farms of Favorita's flagship fruit producer AGRICOLA BANANERA REYBANCORP ABR S.A. are ECO OK (USA) , ISO 14000 (SGS ANSIRAB) y SMART BANANO (UNION EUROPEA) certified. (The last certification is granted by the Rainforest Alliance). Certifications are carried out independent international surveyors.

Any additional questions or requests for clarifications are always welcome.

Cordially,

Dr. Segundo Wong Mayorga
Executive President
FAVORITA FRUIT Co. Ltd.